Journey to Reality

Sacramental Life in a Secular Age

ZACHARY PORCU, PhD

ANCIENT FAITH PUBLISHING
CHESTERTON, INDIANA

Journey to Reality: Sacramental Life in a Secular Age

Published by:
Ancient Faith Publishing
A Division of Ancient Faith Ministries
1050 Broadway, Suite 6
Chesterton, IN 46304

ISBN: 978-1-955890-62-5

Library of Congress Control Number: 2023951540

Cover design by Jannica Porcu

To my uncle Greg and my friend Reggie, who were the people that—in some sense—I wrote this book for, but each of whom died abruptly before I could complete it. If you, dear reader, could pray for them, even once, I would appreciate it.

and

To all of my students who read through this manuscript over the years and whose feedback and enthusiasm helped make it what it is today (you know who you are!).

Acknowledgments

Special thanks are owed to my father and to Fr. Dn. Nicholas Dujmovic, both of whom read through the early drafts and whose encouragement was invaluable.

I am grateful for the support of my clergy and academic peer-reviewers: Fr. Josiah Trenham, Fr. Jason Covarrubias, Fr. David Subu, Fr. Dn. Nicholas Dujmovic, Dr. Andrew Cuff, Dr. Michael Osadchuk, and Christopher DuPée; for those who gave reader feedback: Ben Lin, Caitlin Veneklasen, Christina Jatras, Daniel and Mona Porcu, Daniel Vasquez, Jannica Sophia Porcu, Joshua Cords, Ken Liu, Kristi Shumway, Matthew Yocum, Nicholas Jones, Patrick and Jessica Oberlin; for my student readers (who are many), but especially Brody Derrick, Christopher Partida, Cody Rawson, Erin Brunansky, Giulia Ledda, Gretchen Adrian, Lauren Erickson, Max Kaiser, Rene Wash, Samantha Shaffer, Sophie Sperduto, Cierra Little, Anais Thompson, Ashlie Alshouse, Lexi Morris, and Sienna Santana; the St. Mary's High Schoolers; the eleventh-grade boys of Trinity at Meadow View who helped me flesh out some of these ideas; and for the general and constant geisting of Teddy Laurman.

Acknowledgments

Table of Contents

Part III
Sacred and Secular

Foreword

The most influential book ever written on preaching and teaching the Christian faith was penned by St. John Chrysostom in the late fourth century and entitled *On the Holy Priesthood*. Besides expounding upon the qualifications for ordination as set forth by St. Paul in his pastoral letters, St. John devoted a significant portion of his treatise to the necessary intellectual development of the priest to win the hearts and minds of pagan Romans.

The saint argued that the teacher must possess a mastery of *two* subjects—*both* sacred theology *and* the intellectual mores of the culture he hoped to win to the Christian faith. Today in the twenty-first century West, fruitful Christian pedagogues need to be diligent students of both the gospel and secularism—the secularism that rules our lands.

Dr. Zac Porcu is one of these faithful students who has immersed himself both in the Holy Fathers and in the humanist zeitgeist. As such, he is able to competently assist God-seekers in bridging the gap from the emptiness of post-Christian culture to the mind of the Church. He has assisted me in providing catechesis in the parish, and I rejoice that with the publication of *Journey to Reality* he will be able to help a much larger audience immerse itself in the life of Holy Orthodoxy.

Fr. Josiah Trenham
St. Andrew Orthodox Church, Riverside, California

Introduction

When St. Patrick evangelized Ireland, it wasn't uncommon for the Irish converts to continue some of their pagan practices even though they had converted to Christianity. This wasn't because they didn't believe in Christianity but because it's difficult to change the way you think about the world all at once.

Up until that point, the Irish had been pagan for their entire existence. Paganism was so deeply rooted in their culture that their ideas and attitudes toward the world remained pagan even after they converted. You might say they had been pagan so long that they didn't know how to think about the world in any other way, even when they sincerely wanted to be Christian.

Because of this, they sometimes misunderstood the fundamentals of Christianity while at the same time were unable to recognize their error. This is why they could think of themselves as pious Christians while still, for example, praying to the god of the ocean when they went sailing.

To modern people this may seem like an obvious, even a silly contradiction. But when it comes to understanding sacramental Christianity, we Americans are more similar to those early pagan converts than we might think.

Because many Americans think of themselves as religious—especially as Christian—it's easy to imagine that we already understand something that we may not understand properly at all. In fact, we may be in even more danger of misunderstanding sacramental Christianity than the converts of ages past—precisely because we think of ourselves as already knowing what Christianity is.

It's important to understand that America was shaped by the particular spiritual culture of the seventeenth and eighteenth centuries, a time in which there was a great deal of religious confusion. Many people claimed to be Christian but believed very different things: that wealth and prosperity were the main signs of God's blessings, that God made the universe but didn't interact with it, that Jesus was merely a great moral teacher, or that Christianity was inseparable from certain political movements, to name a few. But these ideas—like most other American religious ideas—would have been completely foreign to the early Church.

Consequently, it's easy for modern Americans to be confused about religion. Even the most well-meaning of people who investigate sacramental Christianity are inevitably influenced by assumptions and attitudes that are incompatible with a sacramental way of viewing the world.

This confusion is just as common for critics of Christianity. Many skeptics, ex-Christians, and atheists have in fact never heard the gospel as it was authentically believed by the early Christians. They have only heard the teachings of various American religions that, while claiming to be Christianity, in fact bear almost no resemblance to the religion of the apostles and often contradict it outright.

This is why the Church cannot simply present itself in a vacuum. It must speak to a particular people with particular cultural backgrounds, tendencies, and attitudes. We must acknowledge that we as Americans have a specific heritage that's been shaped by the religious movements of the modern era rather than a heritage grounded in apostolic Christianity. This isn't to say there is nothing good in American culture—just as we can't say there was nothing good in Irish paganism. But whatever good there was in either, both need the gospel.

To receive the gospel, however, does not mean to *agree* with something called "the teachings of Jesus." The ancient Church did not understand the gospel as a matter of agreement but as a particular way of interacting with reality. You might even say that their whole religious life was about trying to participate in *reality itself.*

This kind of language is not exactly clear to modern Westerners. It sounds vague or abstract, and to some people it might even sound un-Christian. But that is exactly the issue: we have a hard time understanding—or even recognizing—ideas that would have been immediately understandable to the earliest Christians.

If we wish to engage the culture, therefore, we have to speak directly to its issues. We must rediscover the sacramental understanding of ancient Christianity in light of—and clearly distinguished from—the religious culture in which we find ourselves, rather than assuming the two are compatible. Otherwise, we run the risk of believing in Christ but praying to Zeus—and not knowing any better.

PART I

Foundations

CHAPTER 1

What Is Christianity?

The Early Church

Christianity did not start with a book, though you may be forgiven for thinking it did. After all, discussions about Christianity today are frequently centered on the Bible. When people argue about religion, they often focus on whether something is "biblical" or not, and they'll differentiate themselves from other groups by saying that their religion (or their diet, financial strategy, parenting philosophy, and so on) is "biblically based." If you've heard this sort of thing often enough, you might not see anything wrong with it, but this language contains a powerful hidden assumption. Saying that your Christianity is "Bible based" implies that your religion has its *source* or origin in the Bible, as if the Bible came first and Christianity—as a religion—emerged from the reading of the Bible. But if you know even a little of the history of Christianity, you know this isn't how it started.

Christianity did not have its beginning in a book but in a person—the man Jesus. This man lived a life and conducted a whole ministry of preaching and teaching without writing anything down. In fact, the majority of His immediate disciples wrote nothing down either.

Yet Christ's followers continued to preach, pray, and organize themselves into groups of worshipers long before anything like a "canon of Scripture" was established as a standard for all Christians. It would be decades before all the Gospels were written and centuries before all the writings were compiled and recognized as "the books" of the Church (*biblia* in Latin).

Yet somehow the early Christians already had a concrete understanding of what their religion was about—not just as a collection of ideas but as a living thing. This religion was solid enough to endure in spite of almost relentless persecution by pagans and Jews alike, and then to spread across the entire Roman Empire. The thing that was being spread and shared and that captured people's hearts was not a text; it was a certain kind of *life*—not just a "lifestyle," but life of a certain energy or quality. This life began with a particular human person, Jesus, and continued to thrive and flourish in and through other human persons.

To get a sense of this, imagine a family. A family has a certain kind of life energy—that is, a certain way of being in the world, what we would call a "family spirit." If it's a good family, it has a good spirit, full of love and joy, full of people who are hardworking and skilled at their crafts, who love and care for one another, and so forth. This family spirit also includes its shared frame of reference, its inside jokes, and especially its shared history, all of which play a role in making the family what it is.

The thing about families is that you can't become a part of a family just by *reading*, that is, by looking at it from the outside. You could try to study all the family photos, watch videos people had taken, or read their diary entries and the letters they sent each other. If you had a wealth of material to study and you studied very diligently, you could learn a lot of things about that family, and you could try to imitate some of their practices, adopt their philosophies, or even repeat their jokes. This is the sort of thing that recreationists do when they want to reenact things like the American Civil War or ancient Roman battles, to the point of getting even the most obscure details correct. But recreationism is the best you could do through study. You could only imitate this family; you could not become a *member* of it.

But people do become members of families they aren't born into. This happens by marriage or by adoption; it can even happen with family friends. Notice how this exception works. Let's say you marry into a family. At first you may mostly (or only) know that family from the outside—as a group of people who are different from you. But as you participate more in the life of that family, you begin to understand it from the inside. You start to get the jokes, you participate in the traditions, you build relationships with the other members, and most importantly, you contribute something of your own: you add your humor, your skill, and your character to the family. People are affected by who you are. Things you do become part of the shared history of the family. One day you wake up, and it's *your* family; that vital spirit has become a part of you and you of it. This is not an exceptional phenomenon but a very natural thing. It happens to some extent in every workplace, group of friends, and human society in the world.

This is what ancient Christianity was like. It was more like a living family that spread from generation to generation than a rigid adherence to one way or another of interpreting a set of texts. Again, just look at the timeline: the writings that we call the New Testament were not written during the life of Jesus. While Jesus was around and for a long time afterward, the community of the ancient Church was still building its shared history, organizing its members, and acting out its religious life.

It's true that they had a canon of writings, what we now call the Old Testament, but the Old Testament wasn't the *source* of this new Christian life. The Old Testament had been around for centuries, and no Christianity had ever come into existence because of it. Rather, a *man* was the source. He transformed the human lives around Him, and they went on to transform others. People joined this community and became caught up in its life—exactly the way people are caught up in the life of a family.

It's important for us modern people to realize that this was how everything worked in the ancient world. Not only was there no internet, there were no newspapers or even public libraries. Books and scrolls existed, but they were not as available as you might expect because they had to be hand copied and were therefore very expensive to produce. In the majority of situations, ancient people did not receive their information from writings. If you learned something in the ancient world, you learned it orally, by means of someone passing it on to you (and because of this, ancient people were extremely good at memorizing and retaining exact information). In other words, the medium of knowledge was not writing, it was *living people.*

This meant that knowledge was more than just information. It was a whole way of viewing the world and everything in it, much more like an attitude or a mindset. Thus, Christianity was not just a set of ideas; it was a way of life that you learned from other people who were already a part of that way of life.

When you look at the writings that *were* produced by the early Christians, both inside and outside the New Testament, you see this idea at the heart of the way they talked about their religious life. Much of the time they spoke about it vaguely or indirectly, but you will often encounter them talking about something they call "the mysteries." Only in part were they talking about specific ritual or liturgical practices; you will quickly get the sense that what they were really talking about was some deeper, more important reality hidden below the surface.

The early Christians frequently used sexual imagery to describe this reality, commonly that of a bride awaiting her wedding night. This kind of image may strike modern people as odd, but think about it for a moment. Let's say you are a young person in the ancient world, engaged to be married. In the social norms of a traditional society, you would have been allowed virtually no unsupervised time with a member of the opposite sex, so, in all likelihood, your wedding night would be not simply your first sexual encounter but your first kiss, your first real engagement with the opposite sex, and also the first steps into an entirely new life: the married life. Despite the deep desires—physical and emotional—pulling you forward, you would also experience a profound sense of mystery given the newness and strangeness of these things. Words would be of limited usefulness in preparing you for this experience; you could not understand it until you entered into it.

This is the sense in which the early Christians used the word "mystery." They did not mean something that could not be known but something that could be known only by participation, by entering into it and understanding it from the inside—like a marriage, a friendship, or a family. It's no wonder that the term that came to describe this kind of religious experience was "sacramental"—from the Latin word for "mystery." This was the heart and soul of the early Church and formed the foundation for Christianity in the ancient world.

The Modern Problem

Flash forward to the twenty-first century, and you will find that many Christians do not talk about their religion in these terms at all. In fact, you will encounter a variety of very different approaches to Christianity, many of which look nothing like one another. All these varieties, however, can be boiled down into two general types.

The first type is what we might call a "text-based" approach to Christianity (what is sometimes called "fundamentalism"). This is the idea that—as a religion—Christianity has its source in the text of the Bible, and the Bible is the way the religion has come down the centuries to modern man, like a message in a time capsule. In order to be a Christian (in this view), you must read and understand this text and then put its teachings into practice, which anyone can do if he or she has access to the text.

Notice how such a text-based Christianity functions. It is essentially a process of reenactment or agreement with a set of *ideas* mediated through a text. Sacramental Christianity, on the other hand, is a process of *participation* mediated through a living community of persons. It's true that text-based Christians can and do form all sorts of communities that have their own life energy, which they can also pass down from generation to generation. But our question is about the *source* of the religion. What are these communities based on? If the answer is "on the Bible," then they are based on something fundamentally different from what the community of early Christians was based on.

Even setting that aside, a text-based Christianity has other problems. The main one is that the message of the Bible is not as clear as some people make it out to be. If you're familiar with the Bible, you know that most of it is not a series of explicit moral instructions; it consists almost entirely of a mix of historical records (often given in excruciating detail), some poetry, a handful of letters, and records of prophetic visions whose meaning is generally not straightforward. The parts that *do* attempt to be explicit codes of conduct are mostly centered on the rites of temple worship for the ancient Israelites, rites which modern Jews themselves no longer practice and which almost all Christians ignore outright.

If you try to follow the "teachings of the Bible," therefore, you'll face a variety of difficulties. The diversity of genres—from myth to song to prophecy; the disparate authors and styles (not to mention cultural differences, language barriers, and translation issues); and the ambiguity arising from what appear to be changing moral standards throughout the stories make the task far from simple. This is to say nothing of how easy it is for critics of Christianity to pick out passages that are incoherent, self-contradictory, or simply horrific.

The text obviously needs some interpretation, and a good amount at that. But the text does not interpret itself; no text can, because interpretation has to be done by a person. I know this is not obvious to some people, but think about it like this: There are currently about thirty to forty thousand denominations of Christianity. If the text doesn't need any interpretation, why is it that so many thousands of groups can all claim the Bible as their authority and cite Bible verses to back up their positions, while at the same time disagreeing with each other on major doctrinal issues?

I should emphasize that we aren't talking about minor points of theology. There are core doctrinal differences almost everywhere you look, from Protestants and Catholics disagreeing on the role of the priesthood to Calvinists and Arminians arguing over the issue of free will. Or take any number of diametrically opposed positions held by different groups on social or ecclesiastical issues such as sexuality, the ordination of women, or abortion. I know some people want to deemphasize these differences between Christian denominations, but I don't think that's honest. To put it very simply, if these differences were ultimately trivial, why would people feel the need to break off and start their own denominations as frequently as we know they have done throughout the last few hundred years? Yet all of them claim the Bible as their authority. Clearly something is missing here.

Some people have tried to solve this problem by going to the other extreme, toward a second type of Christianity—what we might call an individualist or "progressive" Christianity. This view tends to deemphasize the role of the Bible as central and instead focuses on the believer's individual spiritual journey. Practitioners of this kind of religion emphasize some version of "being a good person" as their main ethical teaching. They are prone to reinterpreting the texts of the Bible or the imperatives of their traditions in such a way as to bring them more in line with contemporary values and modern sensibilities. These are the type of people who say that they believe in Jesus but don't go to church, or that they're Catholic but don't obey the pope, or that they "follow God" but their sense of right and wrong is whatever pop culture tells them it should be.

The problem with this kind of Christianity is that it becomes difficult to see how it is *Christianity*, exactly. You may be inspired by certain teachings, concepts, or even practices from traditional Christianity, but if you decide which parts of Christianity you want to follow and which parts you don't, then the ultimate basis for the religion is *yourself*.

This would be a strange thing to do in any other context. Let's say I read through a book—for example, Tolkien's *The Lord of the Rings*—but whenever I saw a sentence I didn't like, I crossed it out with a pen. Maybe I wrote over certain words, or rewrote whole paragraphs, or cut out chapters I didn't like. If I did this enough (or even at all), we couldn't really call it *The Lord of the Rings* anymore. We could say that it was based on or inspired by *The Lord of the Rings*, but as a matter of fact, it would no longer be the same story.

It is the same with religion. If you only pick out and follow the things you *like* from a religion but leave aside the things you don't like, then you aren't practicing that religion. This kind of behavior was called heresy by the early Christians. *Heresy* comes from a Greek word that means "picking and choosing." A heretic is someone who picks and chooses which parts of a religion he wants to follow rather than following the religion as a whole. As a result, his beliefs may strongly resemble the original religion, but they will have certain glaring omissions or additions.

Of course, modern people are free to make up their own religions or their own versions of religions. I am certainly not going to stop them. But they cannot say that they are practicing *Christianity* in any meaningful sense, still less that they practice what the early Christians practiced.

Shifting Paradigms

While they appear to be opposites, these two views of Christianity—the text-based and the individual-based—share something critical in common: they are both decidedly *modern*. What I mean is that these ways of approaching Christianity would not have occurred to ancient people, and ancient Christians would have had a hard time understanding them—not because either the texts of the Bible or people's individual experiences were not important to them (they certainly were), but because these things were not the core of their religion. For the early Christians, the core of the religion was Christ—not Christ as an idea or as a merely historical figure, but Christ encountered in a specific way, a *sacramental* way.

The problem is that this sacramental way of practicing Christianity is difficult for most modern people to understand. In fact, part of what it means to be a modern person is to have a certain way of thinking about the world that is incompatible with a sacramental way of thinking. I'm going to use the word "secular" to describe this modern way of thinking. We'll explore exactly what that means in a later chapter, but for now I'll just say that almost all modern, Westernized people think in a secular way to some degree—even religious people.

This is not to say that there are no traces of sacramental Christianity left today. Modern-day Eastern Orthodoxy and (as far as I understand) certain older types of Roman Catholicism hold to traditional forms of Christianity, have historical connections to the earliest Christian communities, and practice what they call "sacramental theology." In fact, these are the two largest groups among people who call themselves Christian today. But even within those traditions, it is common for people to have a hard time understanding the sacramental way of looking at the world, simply because the world we live in is so dominated by secular thinking. This is why some people try to update traditional Christianity to fit modern sensibilities—another sign that modern people have no idea what their spiritual ancestors were trying to say.

If we want to understand what the early Christians actually believed or what traditional Christianity is trying to say to us today, or even simply to answer the question "What is Christianity?" we need to understand how the early Christians thought about the world. This is difficult, not because we lack information about the early Christians, but because we lack their *perspective*. You can have all the information you want, but if you don't have a perspective in which that information makes sense, it is useless at best—at worst it will only create more misunderstandings.

How do we learn a new perspective? This is trickier than simply acquiring new information. To understand another perspective means to step outside your own perspective—which means being aware that you have a perspective in the first place. Paradoxically, the things we most deeply believe to be true are the things we think about the least. This makes it even harder to see how your perspective influences the way you view everything.

Imagine if you had to explain the meaning of the word "wet" to a fish. Because a fish is a water animal, it doesn't know what it means to be "wet." Wetness is its whole world. In order to explain wetness to a fish, you would have to explain two things at once: that the world it lives in is a world of water, and that there is a world outside the water made of dry land and air. The fish can't understand this other world of land and air without also realizing that it lives in a world of water. The two realizations go together.

As modern people, we also need to come to two realizations. We need to understand the ancient, sacramental perspective, but we can't do that without simultaneously understanding how our own modern, secular perspective influences our thinking.

To that end, I want to invite you on a short journey. This is not a fact-finding expedition but an invitation to step out of your world and into another world, into a totally different way of thinking. It will therefore require not just your brain but your spirit, not just your intellect but your imagination.

That said, in order to understand sacramental Christianity, we have to encounter the sacraments on their own terms. We have to enter into that life and become a part of it; nothing can substitute for that experience. But in order to do this well, in order to hear what the sacraments are trying to tell us, we must take seriously the possibility that we are more secular than we realize—and understand clearly what that means.

CHAPTER 2

Ultimate Reality

What Is Religion?

One of the most fundamental differences between ancient and modern people is how they think about religion. For modern people, it's very common to think of religion as a matter of personal preference, like any other consumer choice. "My brother loves watching movies," someone might say, "but I prefer video games." Or "My roommate loves rock climbing, but I prefer lifting weights." In this way of thinking, there aren't right or wrong answers; it's simply a question of what works for you. The only standard is, as one woman told me, "as long as it makes you happy." Other people have said whatever "brings you peace," "gets you through the day," and so forth.

While this is a fine approach to some areas of life, to treat religion in this consumerist or medicative manner is to misunderstand its purpose. Ancient people did not treat religion in this way. For the ancients, your religion was not the answer to the question "What works for you?" or "What makes you happy?" It was the answer to the question "What is the nature of reality?"

Understand that this is only partially a scientific question. It goes well beyond scientific concerns such as what atoms and molecules are made out of, how gravity works, or the behavior of quantum particles. Rather, this inquiry is directed at the ultimate questions: What is the meaning of life? Why do things exist at all? Who are we, and what is our purpose?

I know that some people treat such questions flippantly, thinking they are impractical, but that is not true. The question of *meaning* in life is perhaps the most practical question of all, which I think should be even more apparent in the wake of the modern epidemic of depression and anxiety, to say nothing of suicides or shootings. There is a vast, complicated universe out there; what is its meaning? Whatever your answer, everything else about reality—science, history, literature, economics—is bound up in it. That's why it's correct to say that the central issue with which religion is concerned is *the nature of ultimate reality.*

What We Mean by "God"

Because this question is so important, every culture in history has attempted some kind of answer. Curiously, in what seems to be the overwhelming majority of cases, that answer has something to do with a mysterious power, what we call "God" in English. But here is our first difficulty: the word "God" is somewhat ambiguous in our language (and in many others), and people use it in different senses without realizing it.

There are two distinct senses in which you could use this word "God." On the one hand, you could use the word (usually with an uppercase "G") to refer to a single, supreme deity. On the other hand, you could use the word (often with a lowercase "g") to refer to deities that are not single and all-powerful but instead have distinct personalities, like Zeus, Thor, Ganesh, or Amaterasu.

Confusing these two definitions is what leads to many misunderstandings about religion. You may have heard people say things like, "I stopped believing in God when I grew up—along with Santa Claus and the tooth fairy." Or some people ask, "If God exists, where is he?" and then look around with exaggerated incredulity. There was even a prominent scientist who said that the reason he didn't believe in God is that humanity had been exploring outer space for decades and still hadn't run into "the bearded old man." While such comments may seem witty, they only show that the speaker is confused about the basic terminology of the discussion.

To make things clear, let's use the word "god" to refer to entities like Zeus, Thor, or Amaterasu, but we'll use a completely different word for what Christianity is trying to talk about: *arché* (ar-KAY). This is an old Greek word that means "first" or "primary" (as in "archenemy" or "archangel"), but it could also be translated "beginning," "source," or "principle." What's the difference between a god and the arché?

When we talk about "the gods," what we're talking about are particular entities within the universe. Granted, these may be very powerful entities, superhuman in their abilities and the scope of their powers. They may live for countless generations of men. They may even be involved in shaping or governing the world as we know it. But they nevertheless share much in common with us: they have limitations on their powers; they can be slain (as in many ancient myths); and they have all-too-human traits such as jealousy, lust, anger, and pride. But most importantly, like us, they are *creatures*, meaning that they are part of the universe and ultimately dependent on it, just as we are. The difference is simply one of power. Despite their sometimes profound contributions to shaping and governing the world, the gods are unmistakably *in* the world and are to some extent bound by it.

The arché, by contrast, is exactly the opposite. The arché is not any particular being in the universe, in the sense of something we can point to or identify, nor does it exist beyond this universe in some higher universe of its own. The arché is not a *thing* in the sense that you, a dog, or Zeus are *things*. Such things are part of the universe, exist in space-time, are limited in what they are, and depend on something else for their being. But the arché is not a part of any universe, is outside of space-time, is unlimited, and has no source of existence. What this last part means is that, far from being any particular *thing* in the universe, the arché is itself the source of *all* reality and being. It is, you might say, "being itself" or "reality itself."

It's difficult to put this into words, but you can see that's because of the nature of what we're trying to describe. Because the arché is not an object or item in the universe, any analogy we make to objects or items will be, ultimately, inadequate. There are, however, two images that may be helpful.

One comparison is that the arché is like life (in the sense of "being alive"). Suppose you walk into a park in springtime and, on seeing the dragonflies, birds, and squirrels along with all the blooming flowers and plants, you say that the park is "teeming with life" or that "life is in the air." What is this "life" you're talking about? It's true that the park is full of living *creatures*, but there is no particular thing or object you can point to and say, "That there is *life*." "Life" can't be any particular plant or animal in that park, but it is something that everything there has. It's the power or principle in which all of those things share and by which they are able to live. It is the same with existence: there are many things that exist, but the principle or power by which they exist is not one of those things. That power is what we mean by the arché.

A second example is light. Most of the time you don't perceive light directly. You know that light is present primarily because you are able to see *other* things which the light has illuminated. If you are in a completely dark room and suddenly the light turns on, you know the light came on because now you see a couch, walls, a desk, and so on. Light is the *medium* by which you are able to see anything at all.

Life and light are, incidentally, two of the most common analogies that have been used to describe the arché throughout history. The analogies are, as I warned, ultimately inadequate. A more accurate (though more abstract) way of putting it is that the arché is the "ultimate principle of reality." It is that power from which everything flows and in which everything has its being.

The Arché and the Gods

You can see now why the arché is not even in the same category as things like Zeus or Thor. Such gods are actually in the same category as dogs or rocks—that is, specific *objects* in the universe. We can ask the question "Where did Thor come from?" (the answer being something like "He was born of Odin"), but we cannot ask this question of the arché in the same sense: to ask where the arché came from is more like asking where *being* came from.

You might be tempted to confuse this last question with the question "Where did the universe come from?" and think that, because we know how babies and clouds and planets are formed, we are on our way to figuring out the explanation for where everything in the universe came from. But that is a different question. We are not asking how individual objects in the universe came into being—or even how *every* individual object came to be. Our question is about the mysterious phenomenon of existence itself, a question which still could not be answered even if we knew the individual causes of every object in the universe.

There is a sense in which most ancient cultures believed in both the arché and the gods. It's not that ancient pagans (like Greeks or Egyptians) believed in many "divinities" while Christians and Jews believed in only one. Most Greeks would have believed in the arché just as they believed in the gods. And Christians or Jews, while articulating their respective notions of the arché, would also have believed in a whole myriad of superhuman, unseen powers that governed or interfered with the world: mighty archangels, malevolent demons, burning seraphim, austere cherubim, and so forth—in other words, creatures that a Greek would have immediately identified as "gods."

Early Christian thinkers noticed this similarity. Saint Augustine even went so far as to say that the pagans used the word "gods" to mean the same things that the Christians called "angels." He didn't think this was a problem because the lower gods obviously belonged to a completely different category from the one God who is the arché.

We see this distinction in almost all the great religious and philosophical traditions. Though they called the arché by different names—Tiān in Chinese, Brahman in Hinduism, the Absolute in modern philosophy, and so on—they all had a clear understanding of the difference between things *in* the world and that power or principle *by which* the world is sustained and has its being. This idea—the idea of the arché—is what Christians mean when they use the English word "God" with a capital "G."

So then, when we ask about whether there is a God in this sense, we are not asking whether there is some specific superhuman entity that orders or governs the universe. That is thinking far too small. We are asking about the arché of all being: the source, the principle, the thing that is *being itself.* This is the highest and most important of all questions; there is nothing the answer does not affect.

CHAPTER 3

Who Is God?

The Moral Reality of the Arché

There's a sense in which the idea of the arché is not that hard to understand. If you think about it as "life" or "being," then it's easy to distinguish it from deities like Zeus or Thor. Most ancient religions thought of the arché either as some sort of divine substance out of which the universe emerged or as a mysterious force that governed reality—or both.

Many ancient thinkers also understood the arché as moral. The ultimate, cosmic source of all life and being was, they thought, also the source of all morality. In other words, the arché wasn't just reality itself but also *goodness itself.* While they differed on the exact nature of the arché and the extent to which you could interact with it, almost all ancient cultures had some idea of an ultimate source or principle for both the physical world and the moral world—and often they understood them as the same thing. You see the same kind of idea when contemporary people talk about "the universe" in vaguely moral terms: "I think the universe is trying to tell me something," or "The universe wants me to do such-and-such a thing."

The Personal God

The early Christians, however, went a step farther than this. They believed that the arché was also personal. That is, the arché was not just a governing force or animating principle but also a person with a mind and a will. You might think that when I say "a person," we are now back to talking about a certain specific entity in the universe, like Zeus or Thor, and that to say the arché is a person means that some entity in the universe also happens to be the ultimate power. But that is not the Christian idea.

Let's say I bring you a rock and tell you, "This isn't *just* a rock; it's also a person." When you look at the rock, you see that it indeed has qualities you associate with a person, such as being able to think and speak and interact with you. We could imagine the same thing on a bigger scale, such as a whole mountain that wasn't just a mountain but also a person. If you can imagine that, you can probably also imagine that our entire planet could be a person, with its own thoughts and will. You could maybe even imagine that the universe (in whatever sense we can talk about the universe as a single object) could also be a person.

However, this is *not* what we mean when we say that the arché is a person. We're not taking some object (a rock, a mountain, a planet) and adding the idea of personhood to it. We're saying that the ultimate governing principle of reality—*distinct from the created universe*—is personal.

There's a famous story from the Bible that's helpful in understanding this. When God appeared to Moses and told him to lead the Israelites out of Egyptian captivity, Moses asked for God's name so that he could tell the Israelites who it was that sent him. The name God told him was "I am." This wasn't God describing something true *about* Himself, for of course you could say the same thing about yourself. Rather, God was giving His *name*. I know many of our names for people and things can seem arbitrary, but a good name tells you something about the thing you're naming. This is how nicknames usually happen: a girl with red hair gets called "Red," a tall man named George gets called "Big George," and so on. Likewise, the name God gave Moses was one that corresponded with His nature: "I am." In other words, to exist—or better yet, to be existence itself—is God's nature.

The One or the Many?

All right, you might say, so what? Why does it matter that the arché is a person? To understand the significance of this, we have to ask something basic: What do we mean by "person"? As with most things, it depends on whom you ask, and different cultures have given different answers. However, we can categorize almost every answer into one of two general worldviews.

The first view is what we might call a "worldview of the One." This is the belief that all people, and indeed all of reality, ultimately constitute one single being. People who believe this would say that the distinction between one person and another is an illusion caused by our lack of knowledge. If we were enlightened—that is, if we really understood reality as it is—we would see that there is no ultimate difference between any persons or things at all. "All are one," they might say, even if we appear to be different.

In this view, "persons" are like water. Water droplets appear to be separate and distinct, but if you put them together, they merge seamlessly into one pool of water, all their distinctiveness instantly melting away. On this view, the arché is the ultimate source of all water—is water itself—and we individual water droplets have been separated from the arché and are trying to merge back into it. This view was common in the ancient world and lives on today in religions such as Hinduism.

The opposite worldview is what we might call a "worldview of the Many." In this worldview, the primary reality is that of individuals. Distinctions between people are not illusions; they are the main way you know who you are. I am me precisely because I am not you. I am distinct, self-sufficient, and independent of all other individuals, so much so that we might call this view a kind of radical individualism. Individuals can enter into relationships with one another, but ultimately they are their own beings, separate and distinct.

Rather than water droplets, "persons" in this view are more like stones. Each stone is totally distinct from every other stone, and while you can put them next to each other, stack them, or build something with them, there's no way to merge them together as you can with water droplets. You could grind them up and make them into powder, but then they wouldn't be stones anymore. In other words, the only way to get them to merge together would be to utterly destroy their identity as stones. In this view, the arché might be like one huge stone, and we individual persons might be like parts of the stone that have broken off. But unlike water, once you're broken off, you can't merge back with the original stone. You are forever separate and distinct—both from the arché and from all other stones.

Both of these worldviews seem to explain an important element about the world we find ourselves in, but each does so at a cost. The worldview of the One explains, truly enough, that there is some kind of fundamental unity among all people and all things, but it does so at the cost of our individualism. Persons can't really exist in this view: our distinctiveness turns out to be an illusion, as our very nature means that we belong to a greater whole that has no place for our individuality. If a drop of water falls into the ocean, the drop ceases to exist, and there's no way to get it back.

In a worldview of the Many, we get to preserve our individuality but at the cost of any sense of unity. Because (in this view) you don't share a connection with any other person at the level of ultimate reality, there's a sense in which you'll always be alone, despite however many connections or relationships you make. And in fact, this needs to be so in order to preserve your individual uniqueness. Otherwise you'd just melt into other people and disappear—the way water droplets do.

Neither of these views paints a complete picture of the way we experience reality, and still less do they resolve the problem of how to understand the arché as a person. Are all selves ultimately one? If so, then there is no such thing as individual persons; we're all just fragments of one supreme consciousness. Are all selves ultimately separate? If so, then whether or not the arché is a person (or even whether or not any other persons exist) is largely irrelevant, since only *you* as a person matter. You become the center of your own universe, independent but alone.

In order to transcend the limitations of both these views, we need a worldview that can combine the best features of the One and the Many without being either of them.

The Trinity

There is one worldview that does this, and that's the ancient Christian idea that the arché is a Trinity. How and why the early Christians came to this conclusion is a story of its own. If you are interested, you will no doubt look into it more thoroughly. For now I only want to give a brief overview of this idea, and—more importantly—explain why it matters.

The formula the early Christians developed to explain the Trinity is that God is three *Persons* and one *essence*. They identified the three Persons as the Father, the Son, and the Holy Spirit. These three Persons are fully distinct from each other: the Father is not the Son, the Son is not the Spirit, and so on. However, they are not *separate*, because they all have the same essence. Indeed, they share this same essence so completely that we can correctly call them *one God*. One God, three Persons.

At this point, you may (perhaps unconsciously) be creating a simplification of the concept in your mind. People have been trying to do this for thousands of years. "I get what you're saying about three different persons," a Muslim once told me. "But really, the *main* thing is the one God, right?" He was ready to accept the Persons of the Trinity as different "faces" of God or different "roles" that God plays, as long as what we were really talking about was one God. But you could also take the opposite view. You could say that the Father, Son, and Holy Spirit are actually three *different* gods who seem like one because they're always in perfect agreement and always do everything together.

Both of these views are errors, but they're easy to make. They're so easy, in fact, that we often make them without realizing it. We do this by unconsciously prioritizing either the Oneness or the Threeness—even by just a hair. But there are problems both ways. If you prioritize the Oneness, then the Persons disappear and you get one divine Being; if you prioritize the Threeness, the one arché disappears and you get three different gods. Both of these views were rejected by ancient Christians. Their understanding was that God was both One and Many *simultaneously*. But how does that make sense?

One way to understand it is to compare the Trinity to a family. A family is made up of distinct persons, but the members of a family share the same genetic makeup. This is why family members look alike, have similar traits and tendencies, and so on. In the case of the children, they are literally made out of the same biological material as their parents. So there is a sense in which a family, while being made up of distinct individuals, also shares something that is a fundamental part of their being: the medium of their biology. A family is, in this way, simultaneously one family but many people.

Now, just as with analogies to the arché, analogies to the Trinity are always going to be inadequate. The Trinity is not the same as a family because the Trinity has one essence in a way that a family does not. To understand the Trinity more accurately requires a much more technical answer, but in my experience that is not what most people are interested in. What most people want to know is something very simple: Why does any of this matter? The answer is also very simple and very pertinent: If God weren't a Trinity, there would be no such thing as love.

Being and Love

One of the major problems with both the worldview of the One and the worldview of the Many is that neither has any room for love—at least not as we'd like to understand it. In a worldview of the One, where we're all just water droplets, the sentence "I love you" is meaningless, since there is ultimately no difference between "I" and "you." If all beings were one, the universe would simply be one being in love with itself.

The worldview of the Many has the opposite problem. In this view, "I love you" translates to something like "I am having a particular emotional experience of you." Because we're ultimately separate beings, love can't be something we truly share. What we mean by *love* is actually two separate experiences: my experience of you and your experience of me. And if you've ever watched a movie in which someone loves someone who doesn't love them back, you know that these two experiences don't necessarily line up.

The Trinity, however, is the best of both. The Father, Son, and Spirit can love each other because each is His own Person, distinct from the others. There is an "I" and a "you." At the same time, however, their love isn't merely an individual, emotional experience they're having of one another; their love for each other is the *same* love because the three of them share one single essence.

I'm aware that this doesn't make immediate intuitive sense to most modern people, but that's because of the way we define "person." When modern people use the term "person," we mean it as synonymous with "individual." In other words, we unconsciously assume the worldview of the Many, in which each person is a totally separate entity. If that's your assumption, then the idea of three persons sharing one essence sounds like a contradiction.

But the ancient Christian idea was different. For them, a person was—by definition—a *relational* thing. To be a person meant to be defined by your relationships to other persons. You probably have a sense of this already if you've noticed how you tend to be influenced by the people around you. If you spend a lot of time with certain people, you generally pick up their mannerisms, vocabulary, inflections, and even their sense of humor, outlook toward life, or beliefs.

The Christian idea of the person is like this but even more so. The idea is that, at the deepest level of our being, we define each other and even bring each other into existence. You'll notice that it takes two humans to make another human. That's always seemed very significant to me: even your existence you owe not to one but to *two* other people coming together out of a passionate desire for each other. This is an important clue to our nature. Our love for one another, expressed physically, leads to the creation of new human persons. You literally owe your existence to a *relationship*.

A word we might use to describe this concept is "interdependence." Often we can't define one thing without defining another thing first. To understand what a beetle is, you need to understand what an insect is, and to understand what an insect is, you need to understand what an animal is, and so on. But sometimes two things are mutually definitional to one another, like "father" and "son." To be a father means to have a child, and at the same time, to be a son means to have a father. Each term needs the other to have meaning. And, as you may have noticed, "Father" and "Son" are the names of two Persons in the Trinity. The idea that mankind is a single family made up of many members is a kind of faint reflection of the ultimate reality of God's nature, because even the arché itself is a community of interdependent persons united in perfect love.

Love as the Arché

It's important to understand that when early Christians talked about love, they didn't just mean a feeling. Their idea of love was infinitely more solid than that. They saw love as a description of what it means to be a person, of the way we are unified at the most fundamental level of our being, both in relation to one another (since mankind is ultimately one family) and also in relation to God.

In other words, they didn't view love as a feeling at all, but *as a way of being*. What they meant by love was the living, dynamic state of being in which we are both distinctly ourselves and simultaneously united to others. You may have heard a married person say to his or her spouse, "I always love you even if I don't always *like* you." You see that what the speaker means by "love" actually has nothing to do with his or her feelings. "Love" is a description of being both one and many simultaneously.

This is exactly how ancient Christians understood God. One of the most famous biblical passages on this topic is the phrase, "God is love" (1 John 4:8). The author of this passage, the Apostle John, was not using hyperbolic language to say "God is loving"; nor was he saying "God loves you," or "If you follow this religion, you'll feel a lot of positive, loving emotions." He was making a statement about being: "God *is* love," and now you have some sense as to why. And because we're still talking about the arché, that means the nature of *reality itself* is love.

This is the central idea of Christianity from which everything else follows. Many people think Christianity is just another monotheistic religion—one with its own special twist (the divinity of Jesus), but ultimately a variation on the same theme as religions like Islam or contemporary Judaism. The reality is that Christianity is profoundly different from every other religion in history precisely because the Trinity solves this problem of the One and the Many on the basis that God's nature is love. No other religion has ever made a claim like that.

The Trinity is complicated, and people are often tempted to downplay its importance for the sake of presenting a simple, easy-to-understand theology. But people who do this are in fact talking about some other religion than Christianity—usually one they've made up themselves (whether they meant to or not). We're not here to talk about simplified or made-up religions. We're here to talk about Christianity as it was authentically believed and articulated by its earliest followers. And they believed that the arché of all being was a Trinity of Persons united in one essence and existing as a perfect, loving community. That is where we must start, because that's where—for Christianity—reality starts.

CHAPTER 4

The Problem of the Fall

The "Myth" of Eden

When ancient cultures wanted to explain the world, they almost always did so through stories. This isn't because they were unsophisticated or ignorant but because their whole way of thinking about the world was deeply infused with *meaning*. In our modern world, we usually make an effort to remove meaning from our picture of the world. We explain things by appealing to blind processes like the laws of nature and physics—things that happen "just because." This method has allowed us to explain a great deal of *how* things happen in the universe, but it does not help us explain *why*.

The reason is that *why* is a question about the inherent or ultimate meaning of things, a question that is beyond the purview of scientific analysis. In the Greek story of Prometheus, for example, man's use of fire is first taught to him by the titan god Prometheus, who is subsequently punished by Zeus. This story is not really an explanation of how man learned to use fire. It's a narrative about the meaning of reality. It tells us that fire is powerful as well as dangerous and that divine insight is required to discover and invent. If you conceive of fire (or insight) as a divine thing and a gift from the gods, then you're suddenly caught up in a world of deeper meaning. You have, in effect, become part of a living story, with all the thematic complexity, relationships, and moral content that entails. We call this kind of narration *myth*, not because we mean that it's untrue, but because the explanations offered are not just about the *how* (sometimes they aren't about the *how* at all), but they address the *why*, the deep moral fabric of reality.

Notice also that scientific and mythic explanations are not fundamentally at odds with one another, as some people think. In fact, they're operating along two different dimensions. Scientific explanations are concerned with the *how* and never with the *why*, and myth is almost always the opposite. Something could have both a scientific and a mythic explanation, and they would not need to contradict one another, just as the height and weight of an object need not be correlated. And if you have only the height or only the weight of an object, you won't have a complete picture of it.

One of the most common *why* questions that myths address is the origin of evil and suffering in the universe. All ancient mythologies addressed this question in one way or another, and Genesis—the first book in the Bible—explains it in the episode known as "the Fall." You probably know the gist of the story: God created the universe, and everything was perfect; there was no suffering or evil. God made the first two humans, Adam and Eve, placed them in the Garden of Eden, and told them they could do whatever they wanted except eat the fruit of a certain tree. But, unfortunately, a serpent lied to Adam and Eve, tricking them into eating the fruit even though they knew they weren't supposed to. So God cast them out of the garden and put a curse on them so that they would have to work hard for their food, suffer their whole lives, and eventually die. And somehow this also caused evil and death to enter into the world at large. If only they hadn't eaten that fruit!

If you're very familiar with this story, you probably don't appreciate the extent to which it could sound ridiculous. Many people have made fun of it over the years. Evil and death enter into the whole world just because Adam and Eve made one little mistake? And why did God have to be so harsh about it?

People have tried to explain this story in different ways, but many of the explanations aren't compelling. They usually emphasize punishment for a crime, which makes some amount of sense but isn't a satisfying explanation. It certainly doesn't explain why the punishment had to be so severe. In sacramental Christianity, however, there is a much deeper meaning to the story.

To understand what's going on with the Fall, we need to go back to the distinction we made in earlier chapters between the arché and everything else. All things exist because the arché creates and sustains them, since the arché is being itself and all things have their being from it. There are two separate categories: that which is created and that which is uncreated. While the arché is being itself (and therefore can't have a creator or even a beginning), created things are—by definition—entirely dependent on the arché for their being.

The situation becomes more complicated when you give a created thing free will. God created man "in His image," and one of the things that means is that man has freedom. God is Himself a Trinity of Persons, freely giving and receiving love to and from one another. For humans to have the possibility of being in a loving relationship with God (or with each other), they must be able to choose those relationships freely. Freedom is necessary for love. You would not, for example, call someone your friend if that person was forced to be your friend. God gave mankind this freedom, but that also entailed the possibility of our refusing to have a relationship with Him.

However, choosing not to be in relationship with God has certain natural consequences. Note what the serpent tells Eve in the

Genesis story. In trying to persuade her to eat the fruit, he says, "You shall be as gods." This is the real significance of Eve taking the fruit: it's not simply about doing something you were told not to do or even about being your own boss. It's about the desire to replace God with *yourself*, to become your own arché—the source of your own life and being. The deeper meaning of what Adam and Eve did in the garden is that they made a radical break with God, not just by disobeying a rule, but in the voluntary act of choosing to separate themselves from God at the level of their being in order to become their own arché.

One way to understand this is by thinking about how electricity works. Let's say you have a power strip plugged into an outlet in your wall. The power strip has power because it draws that power from the source, in the same way that Adam has life because (like any created thing) he receives it from the arché. Trying to become one's own God is like unplugging the power strip from the wall and plugging its cord back into itself. You might do this as a joke, but it obviously doesn't work, because a power strip isn't a power *source*. Plugging it into itself cuts it off from having any power at all. What happened in the Fall is something along these same lines. Death and suffering coming into the world was less like a punishment for disobedience and more like the natural consequences of humans attempting to change their being in a way that clashes with the nature of reality. In this case, the nature of reality is that created things are dependent on the one uncreated thing, the arché, for their life and being.

This act had many effects. Cut off from the arché, man began to die. Not immediately, but gradually. To return to our electricity analogy, this is like unplugging a laptop or a cell phone from a power outlet. The battery has some power saved up from when it was plugged in, but eventually it will run out. The rest of creation is also affected by this change ("Cursed *is* the ground for your sake," Gen. 3:17). The reason for this has to do with man's relationship to creation. God made man the crown and leader of creation, to guide and cultivate it. (This is why God gives Adam intellectual work to do in the garden, such as naming the animals.) If man is the power strip plugged into the wall socket that is the arché, then the rest of the creation is like a bunch of other devices plugged into the power strip that is man: when the power strip gets unplugged, the rest of those devices lose power as well.

The Genesis story is complex and contains many levels of meaning beyond what we've discussed here. But for the purpose of articulating the core ideas of sacramental Christianity, I want to focus on this issue: the main thing that happened in the Fall was man's voluntary act of separating himself from God, which God permitted out of His respect for man's free will. But because God is the arché, then that act of man separating himself had profound consequences for mankind and for the rest of the world.

"In Adam All Have Sinned"

The first thing you may ask at this point is, "Okay, fine, but if Adam messed up, why do I suffer the consequences as well?" There are two reasons. One has to do with our previous idea about the concept of persons as *relational*. Unlike the worldview of the Many, which defines the self as radically separate from all other selves, the sacramental Christian concept of the person defines the person by its relationships to other persons.

As we noticed in the previous chapter, being part of a family is the main way your identity and your existence are dependent on other people, as you have a shared identity with the other members of the family. How do you identify different people as belonging to the same family? You talk about who is the son or daughter of whom. What it means to be siblings is that you have the same parents; what it means to be cousins is that you have the same grandparents, and so on. In other words, *specific people* are the focal points on which family identity is based. Therefore, if we understand mankind as a single family, then our ancestral parents—Adam and Eve—are the ones who give us our identity as a whole.

Names like "human species" or *homo sapiens* are depersonalized and don't do justice to this idea. C. S. Lewis said it better in his popular Narnia books. The talking animals and mythic creatures in Narnia didn't call the protagonists "humans" but "sons of Adam and daughters of Eve." In other words, while they identified humans as a different race from themselves, they didn't do this by referring to them as having a different *nature* ("human nature" or something like that). Rather, they identified them as having different *parentage*, that is, belonging to a different family. This is the sense in which we are all bound up together with our ancestral parents. Different people, but one family.

Therefore, if something goes wrong with Adam, if he chooses to radically disconnect himself from the arché, it's not just Adam who is affected but also all of us who are "in" him. Adam is like the power strip (the big one, you might say) that is plugged into the wall, and his children are other power strips plugged into him, and their children are plugged into them, and so on, all the way down to you and me. But Adam has unplugged himself and died, and because there's a finite amount of power left in the system, we're all dying as a result.

You see the same sort of thing with a pregnant woman and the child in her womb. If she drinks too much alcohol, takes dangerous drugs, or gets badly sick, the child will also be affected because the child is *in* her and, in an important sense, *of* her. This is how children can have chemical addictions to alcohol or drugs even before they're born: If the mother is an addict, the child develops that addiction too.

And, of course, if the mother dies, so will the child. It is the same way with Adam and us.

Here's a second way you can answer the question. There's a sense in which each of us experiences (or creates) our own personal Fall whenever we do something that goes against the nature of reality, because the things we do affect the people we become. When you do something selfish, for example, it contributes to you becoming a more selfish person. When you act selfishly, you cause yourself to become a more individualized, disconnected person. The issue with doing immoral things, therefore, is not just that you hurt others but that you hurt *yourself*. You have your own personal Fall each time you willfully act in a way that falls short of the true moral nature of reality.

This falling short is what Christians mean when they talk about sin. The Greek word we translate as "sin," *hamartia*, literally means "to miss the mark." When you sin, you miss or fall short of what you're aiming at. Sin weakens your connection to reality and life itself, narrows your spirit, cuts you off from others, and ultimately dehumanizes you. If you know anything about addiction, you know the narrowing and deadening of the spirit that comes with it. In other words, we also have issues when it comes to using our free will to disconnect ourselves from the arché; it's just that we do it on an individual level. And if we're honest with ourselves, we're doing it in little ways all the time.

Adam and Eve and sin are complex topics, and Christians have articulated these ideas in different ways over the centuries. For our discussion now, it's less important to settle on one exact image than it is to understand the main idea. Either we voluntarily separate ourselves from the arché, or else our ancestors did this first in a way that affected all of us, or some combination of both. Whatever the case, the point is that we are indeed cut off from the arché and we do not have life in us. And you know this already: we get hurt, we get sick, we get old, and we die.

The Incarnation as the Solution

Hopefully you have a better sense now of the main issue. While modern Christian rhetoric tends to focus on the guilt and shame that come from sinning, ancient Christians were much more concerned with the ultimate effect of sin, which is death. They were more practical than we are and went straight to the heart of the problem: because of the Fall, everyone is going to die. Even the creation seems to be dying—the sun and all the other stars are, after all, slowly going out. These facts are of critical importance because they threaten to devalue and render meaningless all human experience.

If you've heard about the problem of the Fall, you've probably also heard the common explanation of the solution. It goes something like this: God became a man in the person of Jesus, died on the cross, rose from the dead, ascended into heaven, and promised to return. I don't know about you, but it's not obvious to me why this specific series of events helps solve the problem. If you're used to this language, you may not see the difficulty at first, but again, it's worth taking a moment to appreciate how strange this sort of thing sounds to people who have never encountered it.

The main way many modern Christians articulate this solution—"Believe in Jesus and you'll be saved"—is especially vague and awkward. What does my *believing* in Jesus have to do with the ultimate problem of death? It sounds like a parent waiting for you to say you're sorry ("and say it like you mean it!") before you get your toy back. It's as if death were a problem that God could fix if He wanted to, but instead He's choosing to wait and force you to admit you were wrong. After all, can't God just fix the problem for us, since He can do anything?

The statement "God can do anything" is somewhat misleading. It's true that God has all power, but it isn't true that He can do *anything*. What's the difference? God, being the arché, has all the power there is, but there is no power that can do impossible things. I don't mean unlikely things or things that don't normally happen in our experience, such as somebody walking on water or being instantaneously healed of blindness. I mean things that are impossible in a logical sense. God cannot, for example, create a triangle with four sides, because a four-sided triangle is a contradiction; it's meaningless. It's the same with the old question of whether God can create a stone so heavy that even He couldn't lift it: because it's a logical contradiction, it's really a meaningless question.

Another way of saying this is that the universe has an underlying logic that you can't violate without undoing something else. If you make a triangle with four sides, it is by virtue of that fact no longer a triangle. If you use your freedom to disconnect yourself from the source of all life and being, then death and corruption follow. And if God were to undermine or subvert the effects of human choice, then humans would cease to be free, lose the capacity for love, and ultimately stop being human beings at all.

Therefore, God can't simply wave His hand and fix man's connection with the arché, since there is a certain logic to the universe that we can't undermine without losing things. What needs to happen? Because the Fall creates a critical gap between God and man (so critical that man is cut off from God's life-giving power), the gap needs to be bridged in some way. But there's no way for man to do this on his own: being a creature and limited by his finite nature, man doesn't have the power to alter his being at the level we're talking about. Or, to use a programming analogy, if you write a computer program that can change its own code and it changes its code in such a way that it breaks itself, then it's not in a position to fix itself. Rather, the ability to bridge that gap lies with God.

God the Son, the Second Person of the Trinity, chose to do something radical: to enter into time and become a human being. It's important to be clear about this. It isn't that God took on the outward *appearance* of a human, or that Jesus was a normal human who became so enlightened that He ascended to godhood, or that Jesus was the "perfect person" whom God *created.* Contrary to what some people may believe, these are not Christian ideas. The idea is that Jesus *is God,* but became incarnate as a man—meaning that He took on flesh the same way every other human being does, by being born of a human woman.

People who are misinformed about Christianity think that what's important about Jesus is His moral teachings or His loving disposition, but this is not true. What's most significant about Jesus is that He is both God and Man. This formula is critical. By being both God and man, Jesus creates a perfect link to bridge the gap between God and man within His own being. By being fully God, He is Himself the arché of all existence and is life itself. By being fully human, He gives human nature a direct connection to interface with the arché. God and man are, in other words, joined in one Person. To return to our electrical analogy, Christ not only became a new power strip (being a man) which the human race can plug back into; He is a power strip that does not need to be plugged in, because He is also a power *source.* Indeed, because He is the arché, He is the ultimate source of all electricity—He is electricity itself.

This last image raises certain questions. If Jesus is the new power strip for the whole human race, how do we get plugged in? This is where the whole question of the Church and of practical religion comes into play. But it's also the point where sacramental and non-sacramental Christianity are going to diverge sharply and reveal their deep differences. Rather than jumping straight into the specifics, we first need to take a big step back and get a better understanding of the core, foundational differences between the sacramental and the secular ways of viewing the world.

PART II

The Sacramental

CHAPTER 5

Sacramental Thinking

Physical or Spiritual?

How do you think about the world? It's not really an everyday question, yet your answer reveals a great deal about you and the culture you come from. In fact, when we talk about cultures, or even eras in history, what we're usually talking about is the way certain groups of people think about the world.

Modern, westernized people tend to think about the world from the starting point of physicality. The physical world, we would say, is the primary reality. It's all the things you can taste and touch and see. It is the objective, measurable world on which we can all agree. One thing that unites modern people—whether they are religious or not—is that we are generally comfortable with viewing the world as primarily physical, made up of physical processes and conforming to physical laws. This is what people call the natural world.

If you want to believe in anything other than the natural world, then you have to talk about a second category: the supernatural. When you hear the word "supernatural" you might think of any number of different things: ghosts and spirits, psychic powers and fortune telling, angels and demons, and so on. But one thing they all have in common, in a modern view, is that they cannot be explained by the physical processes of the natural world. While the supernatural world can (perhaps) intrude on the natural world, modern people tend to think of the supernatural as operating on some different level or dimension and therefore as being mostly irrelevant to the day-to-day operations of the natural world.

Because of this perceived lack of relevancy, some people believe there is no supernatural world. What you see is what you get, and that's enough for most people. If supernatural entities exist, they are beyond us in some way that makes belief in them optional, a matter of personal opinion, or irrelevant altogether. Modern people generally have this perspective even if they are religious, and religious people trying to argue for their particular version of the supernatural still tend to do so within this general conception of the natural and the supernatural as two separate domains.

Ancient people (and most non-Western societies today) did not think in this way. They acknowledged that there were both physical and spiritual elements to the world, but far from seeing them as separate domains, they viewed them as *fundamentally interrelated.* The idea is that there is a physical component to all spirituality and a spiritual meaning in all physical things. Ancient people burned incense in their prayer, conducted worship in specific physical locations, and offered animal or grain sacrifices on altars. This combination of physical action and spiritual meaning was an indispensable part of all ancient religion, from Roman paganism to the religion of ancient Israel—not because the ancients were primitive, but because they understood that these two elements of the world—the physical and the spiritual—were not separable.

The main difference they saw between the physical and the spiritual was visibility. They referred to the physical world as visible and the spiritual world as invisible, but they never thought of them as *separate.* In the same way, modern people don't think of radiation, atoms, or gravity as separate from the physical world just because we can't see them. In an ancient view, the spiritual world is like gravity or radiation—it's an intrinsic part of the physical world even if most of the time it's invisible.

Intrinsic Meaning

This idea that the physical and the spiritual are not separable has a few important implications. If we say that the physical and the spiritual have to go together, then what we're really saying is that there is a spiritual quality to everything physical, and a physical quality to everything spiritual. This means, among other things, that physical objects and actions can have *intrinsic meaning.*

This sounds completely strange to our modern ears. For most modern people, the physical world is simply what it is. We like to use the word "just" for things: a tree is *just* a tree, a triangle is *just* a triangle, and so on. What we mean is that these things have no intrinsic significance or meaning. Any meaning they have is something we make up ourselves and impose on them.

But if the physical and spiritual are fundamentally inseparable, then physical things have inherent meaning. I'll give you an example. Let's say you draw a couple of lines on a sheet of paper—perhaps in the shape of a cross. What does that mean? If you see the spiritual and the physical as separate, the shape you drew is just a couple of lines. It might have personal significance for one person but mean something totally different (or nothing) to someone else. It has no intrinsic meaning. But in the sacramental view of the world, the shape of the cross has intrinsic meaning with reference to the Christian story. If the Cross is truly the weapon by which Christ defeated death and evil, then the shape of the cross has more than personal significance—it has *cosmic significance*. The shape itself has power, regardless of whether the person who drew it knows that or not. That's why, for example, in certain traditional beliefs, a vampire is *physically* harmed by the sign of the cross, because a vampire has its power from the devil.

There are countless examples like this from every culture. In European folklore, faeries are physically incapable of breaking their promises. The idea behind a curse is that just by saying something like "May you get sick and never recover," you can actually cause bad things to happen in someone else's life. A blessing operates by the same logic: the blessing of a god or an emperor isn't "just" a few words or a hand gesture; it has the power to change what happens in your life. In the Greco-Roman world, different plants, animals, and even materials such as iron or bronze were understood to have direct connections to certain gods, and you could communicate with those gods better by using the appropriate objects. This is the same reason people believed in astrology: if the planets are gods, then they exert real influence over the world and the things that happen in it just by their presence.

Even in the modern world, despite its general rejection of the supernatural, many people find certain connections between the physical and the spiritual to be intuitive. Take the westernized understanding of karma, for instance—the idea that if you do good things, good things will happen to you, and if you do bad, bad things will happen to you. This kind of logic only makes sense if you assume that the physical and the spiritual are interconnected.

Another way to articulate this idea is by distinguishing between an *enchanted* view of the world and a *disenchanted* view. The disenchanted view is that reality is "just" a bunch of meaningless objects to which we assign meaning. But the enchanted view is that, because of the connection between the physical and the spiritual, everything in the physical world has some intrinsic meaning, whether or not we're aware of it. Even if you're skeptical about things like karma, curses, or holy water, you probably have some vague sense of a deeper meaning in the natural world. The glory of the stars on a dark night, the mystery you sense at the heart of a forest, the profundity of the sea, the energy and beauty of the human being—these are things that inspire us and beckon us. We have a sense of their deep significance even if we cannot explain why.

This way of seeing the world also changes how you might think about life. If everything has some sort of intrinsic meaning, then reality is less like a collection of objects in space and more like a *story.* By this I don't mean to suggest that you should view the world as "your story," in which you are the center of the universe; I mean that your story, and mine, and the stories of everyone you've ever met are all caught up together in a huge, cosmic narrative, rich with themes and bursting with meaning.

While modern people tend to regard this way of viewing the world as biased, ancient people had no such concerns. From the founding of Rome to the birth of the Japanese islands, ancient people always integrated the historical accounts of their cultures' foundations with cosmic myths about the meaning of the universe. If the Japanese emperors, for example, are descended from the sun goddess Amaterasu, they share in her power and authority through their literal, physical blood. Who better to rule Japan?

Let's go back to the Prometheus myth we talked about in the previous chapter. A disenchanted way of looking at fire would be as just a chemical process—that is, as devoid of any intrinsic meaning. But in the enchanted view, fire is a part of reality itself, an image of power and danger, life and death, insight and divinity. And further, this meaning is more than merely something for you to think about; it's something in which you participate. If you were a pagan Greek lighting a fire for the first time, you wouldn't simply remember the story of

Prometheus; you would—in the very act of lighting the fire—become a participant in that story.

Objective or Subjective?

Another important element in this discussion has to do with how we think about knowledge. When you insist on dividing the world into two separate domains—the physical and the spiritual—you end up dividing knowledge into two categories as well. This may sound a little abstract, but chances are you already understand it intuitively.

You've probably heard people talking about the difference between *objective* and *subjective* knowledge. Objective knowledge consists of things you can prove. This includes everything that can be demonstrated through analysis, observation, or experimentation, such as the boiling point of water or how large the Earth's diameter is. You might call this type of knowledge "verifiable." It corresponds to the natural, physical world and is exactly the kind of knowledge we use to understand and exploit nature.

The opposite kind of knowledge is what we call *subjective.* This kind of knowledge includes all those human experiences that cannot be proven or verified. The most common type is what we would call taste or opinion—such as what sort of pizza you prefer or your favorite movie. But modern people also include things like love, emotions, aesthetic experience, religious experience, morality, and meaning in this category.

When you divide knowledge into these two categories, however, it leads to a kind of crisis of meaning. Because the things we think of as subjective can't be proven, modern people tend to think of them (even unconsciously) as less real than things that are objective. But the things we can demonstrate objectively don't have any intrinsic meaning. In this view, there's no meaning in the boiling point of water or the diameter of the Earth. They're just facts.

This puts us in a conundrum. The things we can prove don't give life meaning, and the things that give life meaning can't be proven. If you combine this way of thinking with a view that divides the physical and spiritual into separate domains, then your picture of reality is this: there is a physical world that we can prove and explain but that is inherently meaningless, while all the meaning in our lives is either purely subjective or part of some unprovable, supernatural reality.

Participation

What is the alternative? While it's true that some things are easily measurable (and therefore objective) and other things are merely matters of taste (and therefore subjective), most things are in fact neither. Most things are what we would call *participatory.* This means they *can* be known but only by participation, by entering into them and becoming a part of them—just as we saw with the example of a family.

You see this kind of participatory knowledge at work when we talk about getting to know someone. Everyone knows that to get to know someone, you need to spend time with that person. Reading about someone on the internet, for example, just means learning a bunch of facts *about* that person, it doesn't constitute *knowing* that person. Really knowing someone requires participation, and participation brings with it true knowledge, even though it can't be looked up on the internet. You know things about your friend, sibling, spouse, or child that are true things, but that you couldn't demonstrate to anyone. "So-and-so seems off today," you might say, or "something's not right." When someone asks you how you know this, you might say, "I just know," and you'd be right. Why? Because you are a participant in that relationship.

The more technical way of saying this is that participatory knowledge is neither objective nor subjective. It's not objective because it's not something that can be proven through demonstration, but it's also not subjective because it's not merely a matter of your personal opinion or feelings. It is indeed real knowledge that can be known by anyone who also participates in that thing.

Imagine, for example, a cup with an unknown drink in it. The knowledge of what the drink tastes like isn't something you can demonstrate to someone who has never tasted it; it's something they have to experience. Yet at the same time, the taste of the drink isn't subjective, since anyone who also tastes the drink will immediately know what it's like.[1]

You might be tempted to confuse the question, "What does this taste like?" with the subjective question, "Does it taste *good*?" or the objective question, "What does the taste tell me about what this drink is made of?" Whether you like the taste is subjective; what the drink is made of is objective. But the experience of tasting a drink, especially this particular drink, is neither—it's participatory. It's a real, non-subjective truth about reality that cannot be communicated to someone without their participation. Put more simply: objectively, coffee is bitter and sugar is sweet. Subjectively, I prefer bitter things to sweet things. But it's by participation that I can know which is which, because only through participation can I truly encounter them.

---

1 Several readers have pointed out that some people are born with genetic anomalies where certain foods, like cilantro or ginger, taste like soap to them. While this is true, it doesn't disprove the point; it just makes the example more complicated. The idea that your individual experience can change because of genetic factors simply means that a minority of people experience the world differently than the majority. But those people in the minority still experience the same thing as each other: they all recognize it as a soap taste. In fact, it's precisely because we all know what it's like to taste soap that we're able to identify people with this condition in the first place.

Another way to understand participatory knowledge is that you need to have a personal relationship with truth. Do not confuse this with the idea of having your own personal opinion *about* truth. It is much more profound than that. If God is the arché and God is personal, then the ultimate truth and source of all reality isn't just an idea or a piece of data; it is a *person*. Remember the famous saying of Jesus, "I am the way, the truth, and the life" (John 14:6). He wasn't saying "My teachings are correct" or "My religion is the right one" or anything so basic as that. He meant something closer to "Truth is itself a Person, and I am that Person." To know Him is to know Truth itself, and vice versa. This is why you need to have a personal relationship to ultimate truth, because both you and it are persons. And now that God has become man, you have a medium through which you can interact, because both of you are physical as well.

Personal Knowledge

Let's go a step further. If you think about this idea of participatory knowledge, you may notice it has an essential element: you. You can't learn to understand something from the inside without being a participant in it yourself. You can't have knowledge without a knower. This means that knowledge has a personal dimension, not because it is somehow subjective or up to the determination of each individual person, but because you cannot participate in things without a *you* to do the participating. For you and me to get to know each other, we need to have some kind of relationship, and the two essential ingredients in that relationship are *you* and *me*. Going back to our idea of marrying into a family, *you* have to enter into the family in order to become a part of it.

But this is where things get tricky. Getting to know someone or entering into a family is not always a smooth experience. There is often tension between people, and—if we're being honest—we sometimes cause that tension ourselves. Suppose you are trying to integrate into your new family, but you are an angry person, which causes you to take offense at many things people say or do—despite the fact that no one in the family means any offense at all. Or you may be a depressive person, and no matter how much the family members genuinely like you or want to spend time with you, you end up feeling lonely most of the time because you find it hard to believe that anyone wants to be around you. In these kinds of situations, who you are as a person colors how you see the world. Specifically, your vices, shortcomings, or emotional issues may blind you to the reality of the situation and prevent you from having real knowledge about your new family.

This is something I think everyone has seen in other people to one degree or another. We've all had conversations with someone who refused to (or in some sense, couldn't) see some obvious truth because of an issue like fear, anger, resentment, guilt, past trauma, and so on. This sort of thing is sometimes called a mental block, something that wedges itself in your mind and prevents you from seeing things as they really are.

On the flip side, you'll notice that people who see more than other people generally do so because of some virtue or moral quality. Take failure as an example. Everyone fails at something at some point, whether big or small. The question is how this failure affects us. Some people are very hurt by failure, but people who are genuinely humble can take their failures and learn from them, because they don't have a need to protect their egos or save face. Humility, in other words, enables you to see more. Arrogance, on the other hand, will almost certainly guarantee that you learn nothing.

Compassion is another important virtue that helps you see things that might be difficult to see. If someone lashes out at you or is cruel in some way, a lack of compassion means you will only see that person negatively, as mean or as a bully. But the person who lashes out at you probably has nothing personal against you: more likely he's in some sort of pain or distress, and compassion will help you look past the initial unpleasantness and see the real truth of the situation.

Vices and virtues, therefore, play a central role in our ability to acquire knowledge and recognize truth. Virtue helps you to see reality as it is more clearly, while vice and pain create mental blocks and blind spots that prevent you from understanding the world. The better person you are morally—in a real, deep sense—the better you'll be able to see the world around you.

Put it this way. If the truth is like light, then your soul is like a mirror. If your mirror is dirty, it can only reflect so much of the light. To reflect the light better, to produce a clearer, truer image, the mirror needs to be cleaned and polished, not just a little bit and not just once. The practice of virtue is an essential element, therefore, in seeking knowledge and the ultimate truth of things. Why? Because reality is participatory.

Or, to put it more simply, if you're a bad person, you're also going to be a bad friend. If you're jealous, resentful, petty, or arrogant, you're going to have a hard time building a relationship with anyone to the extent that those impulses control your life. To have better relationships, you have to be a better person. And if Truth itself is a Person, you're only going to be able to know Truth to the extent that you're able to have a relationship with Him.

Summary

To think in a sacramental way about the world basically means two things. Primarily, it means to see the physical and spiritual as inseparably linked, in yourself and in everything. This gives the whole universe and everything in it intrinsic meaning or cosmic significance.

Secondly, it means realizing that we understand most things neither objectively nor subjectively, but by participation. And because participation requires a *you* to do the participating, understanding requires more than just intellectual growth; it actually requires moral growth.

How do these ideas play out practically in a sacramental understanding of Christian life? That's what we'll look at in the next chapter.

CHAPTER 6

Sacramental Being

What Are the Sacraments?

Given the ideas we discussed in the previous chapter, we are now ready to approach the heart of sacramental Christian practice and worship. Remember that we're trying to answer the problem posed in chapter four. The issue is that man has voluntarily disconnected himself from the arché and is now dying. God became incarnate as Jesus in order to bridge the gap between God and man, plugging us back into the source of all life. How do we participate in this? The answer is that we plug ourselves back into Christ through the life of the Church—specifically, through the sacraments.

What are the sacraments? So far we've used the term *sacramental* to describe a certain way of viewing the world, one in which the physical and spiritual are not separable. When we talk about *the* sacraments, therefore, we're talking about certain specific physical actions through which we participate in the spiritual life of the church.

Baptism

Baptism is the rite of initiation into the Church and the sacramental life. In baptism, the priest asks the Holy Spirit, the Third Person of the Trinity, to come down into the water and sanctify it, as Christ sanctified the water in the Jordan River by His presence, giving it the power to do two things: to cleanse the sins of the one who is immersed in it and to give that person what you might call a renewed body. Having a renewed body is, in part, what it means to be a Christian. The old body is linked to Adam and inherits death from him. Therefore, a new body is necessary in order to receive life from Christ.

In our electricity analogy, let's say that not only are all the power strips running out of power because Adam is unplugged from the arché, but the plugs themselves have rusted and decayed and cannot fit into *any* outlets now. Baptism is what cleans and repairs those plugs and allows you to be plugged back into the arché. In a certain sense, baptism is itself the act of plugging in.

Practically speaking, there's no standard, visible change that comes from baptism (though there have been exceptional cases), but there is a change at the core of your being because you are plugging into Christ as your new power source. This is done through a physical medium (water) because the physical and the spiritual are inseparable. Man is a physical creature, and physicality is his medium. This means that spiritual power and spiritual change must also include and work through man's physicality. It's not just that your soul, in some abstract sense, needs cleaning. *You* need to be washed and renewed, and you are a body just as much as you are a soul.

The Eucharist

The Eucharist—also known as Communion—is the heart of sacramental Christian practice. The Eucharist consists of bread and wine that have been consecrated by prayer, so that they mystically become the Body and Blood of Jesus, and are then ritually eaten as part of the church service. This may seem somewhat bizarre to our modern sensibilities, but it's not as weird as it sounds.

If baptism is the plugging in of a person to the power strip that is Jesus, then Communion is the electricity. Here we can expand our analogy: A power strip is not itself the thing that makes your lights turn on or your phones charge; the electricity is. But electricity in its raw form cannot charge your phone. Raw electricity would destroy your phone, and probably harm you, because electricity is not safe. The purpose of power strips, phone chargers, power outlets, and plugs is to *regulate* electricity, that is, to put it in a form (and lower it to a degree) that you can actually use it without being destroyed by it. It's the same with the arché: the raw power of *being itself* needs to be put into a form that you can use, given what you are. The problem is that you are a physical body, and the arché—by definition—is not.

How then do we get the life of the arché into us? Here God operates within our human limitations. The way human beings normally live—the way we are nourished and grow and heal ourselves—is by eating. Therefore, God gives us His life in the same way. He gives us Communion in the form of literal food and drink which is transformed so that it is also, simultaneously, the arché. But God cannot transform food and drink into His own body unless He Himself has a body. Hence the need for the Incarnation of God the Son as Jesus: God takes on physicality so that He can give us *Himself* as physical food.

I know the idea of eating God may seem a little strange, but it isn't that different from how we eat anything else. You'll notice that we don't eat lifeless things like rocks and dirt. If you only ate lifeless things, you would die. If you want to live, you need to eat living things—plants and animals. And if you want to be filled up with *life itself,* then that's exactly what you need to eat.

Marriage as a Sacrament

There is something else that is considered sacramental but may seem normal to you, which is marriage. Marriage—like Baptism and the Eucharist—is another kind of sacramental reality in which the spiritual and the physical are bound up together.

In contrast with sacramental marriage, the secular view of marriage is based on a worldview of the Many, in which each person is first and foremost a sovereign individual and only secondarily enters into contracts or alliances for mutual benefit. This is why modern marriages often have vows or other kinds of promises and are based on the idea of a contract that can (if necessary) be broken.

The ancient Christian view of marriage is not contractual but sacramental. It isn't about entering into some kind of alliance; it's about a man and a woman changing their being and physically becoming a part of one another. Look at the Genesis account of Adam and Eve: Eve is not created as an independent being but is literally taken out of Adam—she is formed from one of his ribs. Likewise, when he sees her, the first thing Adam says is, "Bone of my bones and flesh of my flesh" (Gen. 2:23). In other words, he identifies her as being a physical part of him. Notice the Genesis story doesn't say, "And so a man shall leave his father and mother and form a mutual agreement with his wife and the two shall be of one mind." It says, "Therefore a man leaves his father and his mother and cleaves to his wife, and they become one flesh" (Gen. 2:24 RSV). Obviously this is a reference to sex, but it isn't just a euphemism; it's a description of what sexual union means. A simple image that illustrates this point is that of a lock and a key. A lock and a key are not two different mechanisms; they are two parts of *one* mechanism.

This kind of union has spiritual content. Men and women are very different creatures, something that's been affirmed by the witness of every culture throughout all of human history, as well as by an overwhelming amount of precise biological, psychological, and medical data from the modern era. These physiological differences influence their differing psychology, priorities, and interests. Each sex has its strengths and weaknesses, generally speaking, as well as its own quirks. Such differences turn out to be a feature of marriage. Men and women are incredibly different but at the same time are strongly attracted and united to one another through physical love. For two people to make this work—and to become one mechanism—necessitates a kind of profound humility, of emptying yourself for the other person. Rising to the challenge of being a good husband or wife requires growth in a way or to a degree that would rarely (if ever) be required of you if you were unmarried. This is not to say that you can't experience such growth in other ways, but marriage is one of the most straightforward ways to do so.

Marriage in a sacramental sense is not about you. It's not primarily about being happy or being fulfilled. It's about growing as a human being and entering into a higher kind of life and love wherein you can practice a "One-and-Many" mode of existence that imitates the Trinity. Marriage is about identifying yourself with another person so completely that the other person becomes a part of you, while you simultaneously become a part of that person, such that you really are "one flesh," just in different bodies. You work for, take care of, and help each other while suffering together, hurting when the other hurts, and rejoicing when the other rejoices, not because you feel positive emotions toward that person—this is not about your feelings—but because you and your spouse are the *same physical unit.*

This is why divorce is not a trivial matter in a sacramental idea of marriage. C. S. Lewis said it best when he explained that a divorce is much more like a dangerous operation that cuts a single body into two pieces. Once a marriage has been consummated, there is a physical and spiritual reality to the oneness of those two people, and ending it is not that simple. Ending a marriage means that you are cutting up a single living body. It's true that there were times when the ancient Church granted divorces, but it was rare. Divorce wasn't granted on a trivial basis or because you no longer felt like being in the marriage, for whatever reason. Until very recent history, in fact, it was the case in the United States that you had to sue your spouse for a divorce on the basis of some specific, concrete offense (usually adultery), and a judge was required to decide whether to grant the divorce.

The Priesthood

The cornerstone of how we are able to participate in the sacraments is the priesthood. A priest is not merely a leader or organizer in a Christian community, nor does he lead simply because he's a charismatic speaker, a published author, or the most educated person in the parish. Rather, a priest is someone with the training and the authority to administer the sacraments. Priests bless water to make it holy, consecrate bread and wine so that they become the Body and Blood of Christ, anoint the sick with holy oil, lead the service of the liturgy, and perform last rites for the dead, among many other tasks. They are the ones who make our participation in the sacraments possible.

To return to our electricity analogy, while we all benefit from having electricity in our homes, most of us don't set up our own electrical systems. Instead, a person with special training sets it up for us and fixes it when it breaks down. Because electricity is dangerous, the people who do this must be set apart—they need specific knowledge and training. But they also need certain authority. Because of the regulations and permitting involved in installing and repairing electrical systems, electricians need a license—the secular equivalent of a special blessing—to be able to perform installations and repairs.

It's the same with priests, and it's something we see all throughout the Bible. In the Old Testament, certain people were set apart to perform this role—people like Moses and Aaron. When Christ came to earth, He also chose specific people to whom He imparted some of His power and authority. Those people were set apart and became the leaders in the communities of the early Church, administering the sacraments and conducting the liturgy. Over time, they passed that authority and power to their own disciples, and they in turn passed that mantle on to *their* disciples, and so on, all throughout the history of the Church and into the present day.

This authority and power is passed on through a sacrament called "ordination," which is what turns a normal man into a priest (or other member of the clergy). A priest is someone who can trace the line of his ordination all the way back to the original apostles and therefore to Christ Himself. This succession of authority and apostleship from Jesus is called "apostolic succession" and is one of the main things that gives the Church her historical continuity. This is another example of how the life of the Church is like the life of a family—something that's handed down from generation to generation.

Sacramental Objects

If you view the physical and spiritual as separate, then you may instinctively view much of what sacramental Christians do as superstitious or even silly. Sacramental Christians wear crosses around their necks, put up sacred images in their homes and on their things, and bless food and other objects to give them a kind of spiritual power. But this kind of behavior makes perfect sense if the physical and spiritual aren't separable. In a sacramental view, you can interact with the spiritual world through physical actions (what we call ritual) but you can also give physical objects a kind of spiritual energy or charge.

In the physical world, electrical energy is present everywhere. This is what sometimes causes you to get a tiny shock when you touch something metal or to see sparks of static electricity when fabrics are rubbed together. There are electromagnetic currents moving all through the world, affecting many of the operations of nature. This electrical energy is present everywhere, even if you don't see it most of the time.

This is how the Church thinks about spiritual energy. Spiritual power and spiritual entities are present everywhere, but they can be more concentrated in certain areas or objects at certain times. The most common way this happens is that a priest puts that spiritual energy into an object through a particular ritual—like the water for baptism or the bread and wine in Communion. But it also applies to relics of the saints, sacred images or icons, and the church temple itself. This is why sacramental Christians treat certain objects with more respect and care, because those objects are charged with spiritual energy and have certain spiritual properties.

There are many examples of this principle at work in sacramental Christianity, and there are other specific sacraments in the life of the Church. But more important than listing all of them is the core, fundamental logic behind sacramentalism: the spiritual and the physical are inseparable. If you understand that, then you can start to make sense out of the sacramental life.

CHAPTER 7

The Life of the Church

Why Do We Have to Go to Church?

Modern people often ask, "Why does it matter what particular church I go to?" or "Why do I *have* to go to church? Why can't I just pray and worship God on my own, at home, or wherever I am?" Such questions make sense if you view going to church in a non-sacramental way. From that perspective, going to church generally means listening to inspirational music, attending a lecture on the Bible or related topic, perhaps performing some formalized actions that have religious symbolism, and then retiring to another room for snacks and socialization.

While the content of such lectures or socialization is usually spiritual, in practice these kinds of churches are more like a combination of a social club and a political party. Like social clubs, they organize community events and collect dues (in the form of tithes and contributions), and like political parties, the primary thing that gives them their identity is agreement with a set of beliefs—especially the pastor's beliefs.

While these things can be good, they are not the primary focus of church in a sacramental view. Sacramentally, the purpose of attending church services is to participate in a *higher spiritual reality*.

The Divine Liturgy

How is it possible to participate in a higher spiritual reality? As we've seen, in a sacramental view of the world, nothing is "just" physical. Objects and actions have intrinsic, spiritual meaning. Everything is participatory. If you dress up as a superhero, for example, you're participating in that character's spirit, and you can have a certain effect—perhaps an inspiring effect—on other people. You're able to do this because, by dressing up as that character, you are in a sense borrowing that character's energy.

This is why masks are used in many cultures as a way for people to participate in spiritual realities. In Japanese cultural festivals, for example, people often wear masks depicting various demons or spirits, and by doing so they are able to participate in the energy and meaning of those entities. This makes sense when you think in an enchanted, sacramental way: if the physical and spiritual can't be separated, then imitation is always participatory.

Let's contrast this to the way modern people think. Because modern people don't see any necessary connection between the physical and the spiritual, we think we can imitate something physically without any spiritual implications. Even if someone puts on a mask of a god, we would say "It's just a mask," or "It's just pretend." But in a sacramental view, because the physical and spiritual are inseparable, to imitate something physically is also to imitate it spiritually. You can't participate in something physically without also participating in its spiritual meaning.

The same thing can happen in a church service. For sacramental Christians, church isn't just music and a lecture. It's a different kind of thing altogether, what's called a *liturgy* (or "mass" in the West). A liturgy is a kind of group performance wherein certain physical actions are taken together that have specific spiritual content. You might call it a group ritual. The goal is to imitate, and therefore participate in, a spiritual reality through the physical ritual. And the spiritual reality that sacramental Christians are trying to imitate through their liturgy is nothing less than heaven itself.

One of the things we know about heaven from the Bible and the writings of the saints is that there seems to be a kind of angelic liturgy constantly being performed around the throne of God. What this means exactly isn't entirely clear, but it seems there is a grand, cosmic order to reality that resembles a dance or musical masterpiece. If you look at the huge and beautiful dance of the planets in our solar system or in the galaxies at large, it's easy to see a rhythm to the universe. A sacramental way of looking at this is that the stars and planets are not just lifeless balls of gas and rocks, but are—or are governed by—angelic powers. There's a reason all ancient cultures viewed the planets as gods. And we know from the Bible and the writings of early Christians that they understood the angelic powers as being physically involved in the order and harmony of the created universe.

The Old Testament recounts how God taught Moses this spiritual reality, and also how to participate in it. God instructed Moses in correctly building a temple and performing a liturgy on earth that imitated this heavenly, cosmic liturgy. The early Christians (who were mostly Jews) inherited this knowledge and built their liturgy on it. The liturgy used in sacramental Christianity today is a continuation of the very same liturgy that God taught Moses. This is why sacramental Christians call their liturgy the "Divine Liturgy." To participate in it is also to participate in the *exact same* cosmic liturgy that the angels perform around the throne of God. This participation links the earthly and the heavenly liturgy and means that when you step into a sacramental church space that's correctly imitating the heavenly liturgy, you are stepping into a small bit of heaven itself—you are participating with the angelic powers in a higher spiritual reality.

Because of this, the liturgy has a kind of timeless, eternal quality. Some people describe this as being "outside of time," but it's better to say that in the liturgy, all time is present.

This means a few things. First, it means that all the liturgies that have ever been performed are really the same liturgy, since they all equally participate in the one cosmic liturgy in heaven. When you participate in the liturgy, you are, in that moment, participating alongside everyone else who has ever participated in the liturgy all throughout history, because all of them participate in the same eternal present.

Second, Communion—which is at the center of the liturgy—also has this timeless quality. Jesus is a Man with a physical body, but He is also the divine Son in the Trinity. He too exists eternally, and so everyone who takes Communion is eating the same thing. If you take Communion today, it's the same Communion your fellow Christians took in the twelfth century in Russia, the eighth century in Greece, or the first century in Judea.

It's important to be clear about this. It's not that Christians attend many different services in many different places, all of which they call liturgy, and eat many different meals, all of which they call Communion. That is thinking only physically. When you think sacramentally—when you see the physical and spiritual as the same—you understand that even though the church buildings and the bread or wine are physically different at first glance, their participation in the cosmic liturgy and the Body of Christ means not only that their spiritual content is the same, but that their physicality in fact becomes the same as well.

This creates a radical unity among Christians. All sacramental Christians in all places and all times participate in the same eternal liturgy. And we all participate in the same meal that puts the life of the one and only arché into us. The language St. Paul and the early Christians used for this is that when we participate in the sacraments, we have "put on" Christ (Gal. 3:27). We have, in fact, *become* Christ and, in doing so, become a real, living part of the arché. This reality connects us across all space and time much more profoundly than can mere agreement or social association.

You can see how this act of divine participation is totally different from a non-sacramental view of church. The non-sacramental view is primarily about education and socialization. While these can be beneficial, and while there's no reason people can't have beneficial spiritual experiences in these contexts (or in any context), the *goals* of these two types of church service are not the same. Only in the Divine Liturgy is the goal to imitate the cosmic liturgy of the angels and thereby participate in a higher spiritual reality.

Liturgical Time

Part of the answer, therefore, to the question of why you can't just worship at home or pray wherever you are has to do with what the liturgy is. While it's good to pray in your own home (or anywhere, for that matter), the liturgy has to be done in a particular way in order to correctly imitate the divine, cosmic liturgy and thereby participate in it.

But the liturgy isn't limited to a particular church service you attend. It's not as if you go to church, participate in the Divine Liturgy, and then leave and go about the rest of your week, as though you had your spiritual day on Sunday and the rest of the days were normal. Sacramental Christianity is not just about doing a particular set of actions; it's a whole way of life. One way to describe this life is as participation in what the Church calls "liturgical time."

The Church has what's called a liturgical calendar, which includes all the special feast days and fast times of the Church. In the West, Christmas and Easter are the most famous of the major feast days, while St. Patrick's Day and St. Valentine's Day are perhaps the most famous saints' days. But in fact, every day of the year is dedicated to some particular saint, event in the Church's history, or fasting period. Like the secular calendar, the church calendar has different seasons throughout the liturgical year, and these different seasons and feast days are commemorated by changes in the way the liturgy is conducted. Participation in the liturgy, in other words, also means participation in a whole cycle of liturgical seasons throughout the year.

It's important to understand that these seasons and holidays (holy-days) are not just remembrances of the past. When you celebrate a secular holiday like President's Day or the Fourth of July, what you're mainly doing is remembering some event that happened a long time ago. But all times are present in the liturgy. So while the Church might technically be remembering a past event—such as the life of St. Patrick or the Birth of Jesus—sacramentally what we're doing is participating in it directly, in the present. On Easter or Christmas, we don't say "Christ was risen" or "Christ was born." That would be the normal thing to say if all we were doing was remembering the past. Instead we say "Christ *is* risen" and "Christ *is* born," because we aren't just holding memorials of these events; we're participating in them *now* through the eternal present of the liturgy.

The Life of the Church

You can see now why going to church in and of itself is not the focus in sacramental Christianity. It's not as though mere church attendance makes you a Christian. That's how secular things work: you sign up for something and go to the meetings, and that's what it means to be a member of that thing. But to be sacramental is not merely a matter of attendance, nor is it merely about thinking in a certain way or performing certain ritual actions; it is a lifestyle. All worldviews, if taken seriously, turn into lifestyles. In the case of sacramental Christianity, going to church and participating in the sacraments is about living out the idea that the physical and the spiritual are bound up together, and that you encounter them together through participation—not just in church, but in everything you do and are.

Everything in life is like this. You don't, for example, become a member of a family by going to a specific number of family gatherings at a certain frequency, and then, once you've fulfilled your quota, you qualify as a member of that family. That would be a weird way to think about it. Rather, you become a member of a family because that's who you *are*—that's the life in which you are an active participant. Neither do you automatically achieve the status of "healthy" by going to the gym a certain number of times. What makes you a healthy person is that you've built up an entire lifestyle of being healthy. You can't become healthy by sitting at home and reading a lot of articles about health. You don't become a member of a family by skipping family gatherings in order to sit at home looking at pictures of past family events. If you want to be a part of something, you have to *live* it.

Asking "Why do I *have* to go to church?" is like asking "Why do I *have* to go to family gatherings?" The answer is, of course, that you don't have to do anything. But if you want to become something, you have to participate in it. And in sacramental Christianity, the thing you're participating in is the higher spiritual reality of the arché Himself.

CHAPTER 8

The Bible and the Church

How to Read the Bible

Where does the Bible fit into all this? We've established that the Bible is not the source of Christianity and that the life of sacramental Christianity does not consist primarily of studying the Bible but of participating in the sacraments and the life of the Church. That doesn't mean the Bible has no place or even that it has a lesser place. On the contrary, the Bible is read in every liturgy and in all the other services of the Church, informs how church temples are built, and otherwise saturates the whole life of the Church in more ways than you can count. In fact, it has been said that Christian life cannot be understood outside the imagery and language of the Scriptures.

How then should we understand the Bible? Let's start with what the Bible is not. The Bible is not a scientific or historical document in the particular sense that modern people mean this. It's important here to distinguish between *truth* and *fact*. Facts are those things that are objectively verifiable—the boiling point of water, the diameter of the Earth, and so on. But even though facts are verifiable, as we saw previously, they contain no deeper meaning. Truth, on the other hand, includes facts but goes beyond them to encompass the deeper meaning of reality itself.

As modern people we tend to care only about facts. For the ancients, however, the *truth* was of primary importance; facts were important only insofar as they served truth. This is why the Bible is seemingly full of contradictions at the factual level. The Gospel accounts, for example, contradict each other frequently. The order of events, such as Christ's temptations in the wilderness or what is said by the thieves crucified with Him, is different depending on which Gospel you read. Why? Because the authors were making different kinds of points or had different emphases when writing their accounts, and they moved the facts around to support those points. This does not make the Bible unreliable. This was a universally accepted writing practice in the ancient world, but it's baffling to modern people because we privilege fact over all other categories, even over meaning.

So what makes the Bible holy? It's certainly not, as some people believe, that the Bible is a book of foundational, absolutely true *facts* about the world and that its holiness is a guarantee those facts are correct. There are plenty of mistakes and errors in the Bible that have been thoroughly documented. Muslims, for example, often attack the Bible from this direction, pointing out the many manuscript variations and textual errors. But both the Muslim critic and the fundamentalist Christian miss the point here. The Bible is about *truth*, and truth is higher than fact. The factual is only one level of what has always been understood to be a multilevel text.

Three Levels of Interpretation

From the very beginning, ancient Christians recognized three levels of biblical interpretation: the literal, the moral, and the spiritual (what they called the *typological*). The literal level of the text is what the text says literally, the plain meaning of the words. In the story of David and Goliath, David was a shepherd who accepted the challenge of a huge Philistine warrior in the midst of a particular historical situation. He was famously outmatched but went in confidently anyway and emerged victorious. As you can see, the literal reading of the text is pretty straightforward.

The moral level consists of the lessons we can draw from the text or that the text is trying to teach us. A fairly standard moral lesson you can draw from David and Goliath is, "Have faith in God, and He will save you even when you seem outmatched or overwhelmed," though there are certainly others.

These two levels are generally easy to understand, but the third level—the spiritual or typological—was considered the most challenging and advanced level of reading. Let's start with *typological*. It's a fancy-sounding word, but all it means is that this way of reading is about seeing "types" in the text. A type is when one thing (an image, character, object, etc.) stands for something else that has a deeper spiritual meaning. A typological reading of David and Goliath is that David is a type of Christ and Goliath is a type of death, the devil, or both. Just as David conquered Goliath and broke the power of his enemies, so too Christ conquered death through His Resurrection and broke the power of the enemy of the whole world.

This is what you might call the deeper truth of the story of David and Goliath. The story reveals itself as a kind of historical foreshadowing (what the early Church Fathers called a "prefiguring") of Christ's victory over death and the devil. If you're familiar with the epistles of St. Paul, you'll recognize that this is how he interpreted the Old Testament. Paul realized that the books of the Old Testament were not just about the history of the Jews but were also full of deeper spiritual meaning about Christ, the Church, baptism, the Eucharist, and the sacramental life. The early Fathers of the Church followed Paul's interpretive lead and continued to delve into the riches of this deeper way of reading the text, opening up a whole treasure trove of previously unrecognized meaning in the Scriptures.

It's important to understand that typology is not allegory in the sense we mean it today. In a modern allegory, we understand that the characters and other elements of the story are entirely fictitious, and their purpose is simply to be the vehicle for whatever point the author is trying to make. But that is not how a typological reading works. A passage from the Bible can be true at the literal level, the moral level, and the typological level all at once. That is, certain things may have happened in actual history, but they are also profound images and types of spiritual realities. Remember how the enchanted world works: things in the objective, physical world (what we would capture with a literal reading) have real spiritual meaning (what we would capture with a moral and typological reading). It's not one or the other; it's both. Things that literally happened in history can have spiritual, cosmic significance—because the entire physical world also has spiritual content.

Other times, however, a passage might lack a literal meaning. The early Christians believed that, while the whole Bible is *true*, not all of it is *fact*. For example, was it a *historical fact* that God created Eve out of a literal rib taken from Adam? Maybe or maybe not, but what's more important than the factual details is the profound truth this teaches us about the nature of men and women. When Genesis talks about how woman was made out of man's rib, while at the same time all men are born of women, the point is about the true relationship of the sexes—namely, that they are not separable but are intrinsically, physically, a part of one another.

Another famous passage critics often point to is Psalm 137:9, which reads, "Happy is the one who seizes your infants and dashes them against the rocks" (NIV). If you take only the literal meaning of this passage, it seems to endorse murdering babies. But of course, this is an important example where we need to go past the literal level of the text. The traditional interpretation of this passage is that it does not have a literal meaning, only a moral or typological one: it's about taking your sins and killing them in your heart while they are "infants," before they grow up and take over your soul. Perhaps this seems like a crude, bronze-age image to a peaceful society like ours, but the spiritual message is nevertheless true: you should cut off a vice or sin while it's still in its infant stages, before it has the chance to become a deep-rooted habit or addiction.

Acquiring the Mind of the Church

But how do you know which passages in the Bible have a literal meaning and which don't, or which have both? How do you know what the correct typological meaning is? Most people would say that, as with any book, you need to read the Bible in its proper historical and cultural context, and that's certainly true enough. But the higher and more profound context is the *spiritual context* of the Bible—namely, the Church herself, that is, the "family" of historical Christianity.

The early Christians, and those Christians today who are directly descended from them through apostolic succession, are the ones who are most qualified to do this interpretation. There are many reasons for this, but the most basic one is that a family is generally the most qualified to interpret and understand its own history. Because I am a part of my family, I not only am familiar with its history and its life, but I also know the people in my family personally. If you were to read my grandmother's diary, there would no doubt be a lot that you could understand and follow, but there would be many things that you as an outsider would not understand, and because of this ignorance, you might not even realize when you were misunderstanding them. But I, who knew my grandmother personally, would be much more qualified to read and interpret her diary. It's the same way with the Bible. To really understand the deep, spiritual meaning of the text, you need to be part of the family of the Church and steeped in its life. When you are, all sorts of profound meaning becomes available that you couldn't see before.

This process of being steeped in the life of the family is what sacramental Christians call "acquiring the mind of the Church." This doesn't mean agreeing with doctrine or memorizing Bible verses. If that's all you did, you'd have an abstracted, overly intellectualized religion and would never get much beyond the literal level of interpretation. What it means to acquire the mind of the Church is to treat Christianity in a participatory way. When you're a part of a family, you all share a certain family spirit. You think and feel the same way together. When you've acquired the mind of the Church, you have a sense of what's an authentic part of her life and what is not, rather than a set of intellectual checklists. Not that there's anything wrong with the intellect, but having a sense or an instinct for something is a sign that it's gone past the level of intellectual agreement and become a part of your being.

You see this with people who have become experts at a sport, a skill, or a game. My grandmother rarely used recipes when she cooked—not because she disapproved of them, but because her expertise was so deep-seated that it had become instinct, to the point that she didn't even use measuring cups in certain situations. She knew how much of an ingredient was needed just by looking at it. Likewise, in sports or games, expert players report that some of their best plays didn't come from perfect calculation but from instinct—not instinct as a random impulse, but instincts that are trained by thousands of hours of practice, of getting a *feel* for the game.

You can acquire a spiritual instinct in the same way. You can immerse yourself in the life of the Church, participate in the higher reality of liturgical time, and partake of the sacraments. Just as with practicing a sport, when you do those things enough, you acquire the mind of the Church and can think as she does. This is why the Bible and the Church have to go together as two things handed down to us that are inseparable. To really read the Bible with the mind of the Church requires that you have a certain kind of formation—not just intellectual but spiritual.

And just as you can't really understand the Bible's true depths without participation in the life of the Church, so too the whole life of the Church is crafted out of imagery from the Bible. People think that ancient churches relied heavily on music and paintings because most ancient people were illiterate, but this was not the main reason. The main reason is that the life of the Church is inseparable from the imagery of Scripture. In the liturgy, the psalms are sung and chanted in the same way the Torah was chanted in the old Jewish temple. The walls are adorned with images from the biblical narratives. And the form of the liturgy itself calls people to participate experientially in a spiritual reality using all five senses: you see and touch the iconography, you smell the incense, you hear the chanting, and you taste Communion. The Bible, in other words, is not merely read or memorized but lived and experienced. Or, to put it another way, being reconnected with the arché is not something you do only in your mind. It's a new kind of life, and it must therefore be *lived*.

CHAPTER 9

Cosmic Revolution

The Problem of Evil

In order to understand the ultimate purpose and destiny of humanity in a sacramental view of Christianity, we have to address one of the main problems people tend to struggle with in their religious thinking: the problem of evil and suffering.

Every worldview has had to make some sense of this reality—that we live in a world which contains much that is good and beautiful but also much that is wicked and ugly. This odd incongruence, classically called the "problem of evil," is one reason people have argued that there is no God. This problem is expressed in many forms, but the most common one is, "If God is supposed to be all-loving and all-powerful, why does He allow evil and suffering in the world?" The idea is that if God is loving, He would not like to see His creatures suffer, and if He is all-powerful, surely He would be able to do something about that suffering. So the fact that there is suffering and evil in the world seems to be incompatible with the existence of a good God—or a God at all.

There are two answers to this problem. The first is that if you say evil exists at all, this implies a real (rather than a merely personal) standard for morality. In other words, when you call something *evil*, you're not simply saying that thing is inconvenient or unpleasant, or that you don't like it. To call something *evil* is a different kind of claim: it's an appeal to a real, universal standard of right and wrong, what is classically called the moral law.

The moral law denotes something higher than anyone's preference, any kind of utilitarianism, or even the consensus of a culture. "Human flourishing" or "evolved altruism" or "you wouldn't like it if someone did that to you" or "we all agree on these values" aren't cases for absolute moral values and duties, only circumstantial reasons that we don't approve of certain behaviors or that such behaviors are counterproductive to the goals of our society. If there is a moral law, on the other hand, that means there are moral truths in an absolute sense, at the highest level of reality. Without an absolute moral law, all moral statements break down into something like "That kind of behavior is counterproductive to such-and-such agenda." Even if that agenda is to reduce suffering, it's still a relative value and not an absolute one.

The only way you can have a moral law by which you can say that something is really *evil* (as opposed to merely unpleasant or counterproductive) is if there's a moral reality that is higher than, and independent of, all our opinions and preferences. To put it another way, there can only be a universal moral law if there is a universal moral lawgiver, that is, an absolute source for goodness—which is exactly what the arché is.

This is why the claim that something is truly evil implies an ultimate moral reality. If real evil exists in the world and is identifiable as such, that means there has to be an ultimate or absolute moral standard for reality. The existence of evil, therefore, is actually an argument in *favor* of the existence of God, not against.

Where then does evil come from? This gets us to the second answer. The Christian answer is that evil has its source, not in God, but in free will. God gave His creatures freedom because freedom is necessary for love. We all know that if you force someone to love you, that isn't really love. Love requires freedom. But if people are *truly* free, they also (by definition) have the freedom to do bad things and to hurt each other.

There aren't two ways about it. Either people are free or they're not, and if they're free, they're free to do evil. Think of a small child. You tell it not to touch a hot stove, but it exercises its free will to do so and gets burned. Tying the child's hands behind its back might take away the possibility of getting burned, but it also takes away the child's freedom. In the same way, if God wants to allow free will, He has to allow for the possibility of suffering and evil.

For many people, these two answers are sufficient to show that the classical idea of God is *not* incompatible with the existence of suffering and evil. Likewise, the consensus of philosophers and theologians over the centuries has been that these answers definitively show that there is no logical problem of evil. No atheist in history, to my knowledge, has ever provided a good refutation of these answers, despite the sometimes extravagant hypothetical situations people come up with to try to show otherwise.

However, the majority of people, whatever they say, are not really bothered by the *logical* problem of evil. Most people are bothered by what we might call the *emotional* problem of evil: an all-loving God permitting the existence of suffering and evil doesn't sit right with us in some way that's difficult to articulate. It definitely seems there's something missing here. The explanation about free will is satisfactory, but a robust answer to the problem of evil and suffering needs to be more than a refutation of the logical problem of evil.

The missing piece is, I think, our *response* to the reality of suffering. Unfortunately, the response of many modern Christians to the problem of suffering has been underwhelming, to say the least. The worst thing I've heard people say is something along the lines of "This is all part of God's plan," meaning that God uses suffering or evil to accomplish His goals. Though this may sound nice, it's actually a horrible thing to say. While it's true that God can turn evil and suffering into good, evil cannot be a part of God's *plan*, because that would make God the *cause of evil*. God would therefore be either evil Himself or else beyond good and evil in such a way that He would be amoral. In either case, we could no longer be talking about the arché.

Most people don't say this sort of thing, of course. They'll instead phrase it as "God permits evil and suffering because there's some greater good He can achieve through suffering. Our role is simply to endure the suffering and have faith that God's going to work everything out in the end." There are some elements of truth in this answer, but it's still problematic. For one thing, it has the wrong emphasis. If taken the wrong way, such an attitude threatens to make Christianity into a religion of blind obedience, intellectual disengagement, and passivity. As you might expect, the early Christians had a very different response to suffering.

The Christian Response

If the modern Christian response is something like "put up with suffering," then the ancient Christian response could be paraphrased as "transcend suffering." The idea is that all the suffering and evil in the universe can ultimately be overcome. I'll give you an example. Very young children appear to suffer immensely from things that are trivial for adults. If a toddler becomes tired, most often he will begin acting out, crying, melting down, picking fights, or generally becoming cranky, depending on the child. The child's pain leads to bad behavior because he cannot handle it. On the other hand, a mature adult (for example, the child's mother) has the ability to be tired without being undone by the experience. She can endure the pain or fatigue better because of her maturity. She might say, "Oh, I'm fine, I'm just a little tired," whereas a toddler might instead throw a tantrum. The difference here is one of maturity. The adult has the ability to be bigger than any particular suffering that might seem to cause unbearable agony to the child. And even among adults, there is a spectrum of maturity. More mature people can endure more. They don't complain, throw tantrums, or lash out. It's not that they've *eliminated* suffering—they still feel tired or experience pain—it's that they've become bigger than their suffering.

The ultimate picture of this is Jesus. Jesus was essentially tortured (look up "scourging" if you want some idea of the intensity of His suffering) and then killed. Yet the pain did not undo Him or even embitter Him: during the ordeal He famously said, "Father, forgive them, for they do not know what they do" (Luke 23:34). But more astounding than this, Christ was not even defeated *by death*: He came back from the dead and, in doing so, overcame death itself.

Ever since then, there has been a whole procession of men and women who followed Christ's example of heroic confidence in the face of suffering. It wasn't something they put up with but something they transcended. There are perhaps no more poignant images than those of the martyr saints in the early centuries of Christianity who were murdered for their faith. Saint Paraskevi, for example, was boiled alive in oil but was miraculously unharmed by it and then released by her astonished persecutors. Saint Lawrence, while being roasted on a hot gridiron, far from being undone by the pain, was reported to have taunted his torturers by saying, "Turn me over, I'm done on this side!"

Numerous saints have appeared to people throughout history, giving advice, insight, or working amazing miracles—even centuries after their deaths. There have been cases where the bodies of saints miraculously smelled like perfume and incense, rather than rot and decay, after they died. Some have even resisted decomposition for decades after their deaths—without any form of embalming or preservatives. Such miracles bear witness to the human person's ability to participate in Christ's overcoming and conquering of death and evil.

This is the point Christianity is making. Being connected to the arché means that you are plugged directly into *life itself*, making you so alive that you become bigger and stronger than all suffering and evil, even stronger than death. The courage of the saints, their inability to be broken by torture, and their conviction that even death could not take their ultimate life away are all witnesses to this core idea of sacramental Christianity: that no matter how terrible the wickedness of evil, suffering, and even death appear to be, these things can and will be transcended utterly.

People generally have one of two reactions to this picture of Christianity. One is to find it profoundly beautiful, and if that's your reaction, then you have begun to understand what Christianity is really about. But the other reaction is to find the whole thing ridiculous or detestable. It's absurd, you might say, to compare something like enduring the concentration camps with a toddler being tired: being in a concentration camp is *real* suffering, and creating them is *real* evil. You can't get over real, explicit, adult suffering the way a child grows up and learns to control his emotions. To even suggest this, you might say, trivializes real suffering.

To this I would like to say two things. First is, "Why not?" We know that suffering isn't a supreme power before which we are utterly helpless. There are stories from all over the world and all throughout history of people enduring and overcoming profound suffering for the sake of some greater good. I gave the examples of the martyred saints, but even in our own age, there are people who have not only survived terrible experiences but have become better because of them. They have had spiritual insights, written books, and even achieved something resembling an enlightenment experience precisely because they were able to face suffering and evil and transcend them.

Indeed, monks across all the great religious traditions voluntarily subject themselves to unnecessary pain, hunger, sleep deprivation, and other hardships in order to have the opportunity to grapple with suffering and overcome it. And, even at the everyday level, the stories that most resonate with us tend to be about people who have experienced and overcome great hardship, becoming better people than they were before. All these instances are important data points in humanity's encounter with suffering and evil. They tell us that suffering and evil do not have the ultimate power or final say in the universe. The fact that anyone at all has overcome evil in this way, let alone so many people across different times and cultures, is a witness to the power of good in the face of evil.

And good and evil are precisely what all this is about. This is the second thing. If you are against this idea that people can overcome suffering and evil by getting stronger than them, and if you want to insist on the power of suffering and evil, then it seems to me you're ultimately saying that evil is greater than good. This is what the whole issue comes down to: either good is greater than evil, or evil is greater than good. If good is greater than evil, then evil and suffering and misery can and will ultimately be overcome, will be swallowed up by good. If, on the other hand, you think that these few heroic people are anomalies or exceptions and that, on the whole, mankind cannot transcend suffering and evil, then you have to believe something else: either that evil is greater than good, or that the universe is meaningless and the only reality is suffering and darkness.

But if you want to say the universe is meaningless, understand what that entails. It would mean that all the beauty and joy in the world—all music, poetry, art, storytelling, love, and play—isn't real but an illusion. You'd have to say that the kind of beauty that pierces the soul, the music that brings you to tears, or the joy you experience in your most ecstatic moments has no genuine relationship to reality but is only some sort of illusion, devoid of any ultimate meaning. There are two problems with this conclusion.

First, it's problematic from a basic scientific standpoint. In science, the best theories are those that most adequately explain as much of the data as possible. Scientists call this the explanatory power of a theory, and they prefer the theories that have the most explanatory power—that is, those that are able to explain as much of the data as possible. Coming up with an overly simplified model that requires you to discard or ignore lots of data is a bad way to explain anything. To propose that there is no meaning at all in the universe is to throw away most of the data of human experience, across every culture and time period, as illusory. For again, every culture in history has had some conception of the good, of absolute moral values, of some kind of arché of all being and all goodness. And every culture has had an acute sense of beauty and has made art accordingly. These realities have to be taken seriously, just in the name of good science.

But there is a more profound logical problem with saying the universe is meaningless. If the universe were truly meaningless, we would never have been able to discover that. To go back to our analogy about the fish, if the whole universe were underwater and there was no dry land anywhere, the word *wet* would have no meaning. There would be no dry land to escape to in order to look down and say, "Those fish are wet." And if the whole world were only water, no one would ever be able to discover what the word *wet* meant. It's the same with meaning.

If everything were truly meaningless, how would we ever have gotten the idea of meaning in the first place?

Good and Evil

What then do we mean by good and evil? It's important to understand that we aren't talking about *opposites*. Some people think you can only tell what's good and what's evil by contrasting them with one another, and this leads people to speculate about whether good or evil is greater. But debates like this don't take into account the most important question: What is real?

What Christianity is saying is that goodness is also *reality*. Remember that the arché is not just reality itself but also goodness itself. Evil, therefore, is a falling away from both the reality of the arché and the goodness of the arché. Another way to say this is that if goodness is ultimate reality, then turning away from the good is also turning away from reality.

This means that evil is not a thing in itself but only a corruption or a privation of reality. Take a minute to think of all the bad things in the world, and you'll notice that every bad thing is just a corruption of a good thing. For example, you might say that rape is a bad thing (and that's true), but rape is better understood as the *misuse* of sex, which is itself a good thing. Violence may seem inherently bad, but what we mean by violence is the misuse of physical force, which is a good thing that we use all the time, from cutting an onion to hammering a nail. Indeed, the exertion of intense physical force is precisely what gives all the joy and excitement to things like sports and martial arts. Hatred might seem inherently evil, but it too is simply a misuse of something good—namely, passion or spirited emotion.

The way the early Christian thinkers explained it was that evil cannot be a thing in itself the way goodness is a thing in itself. You can be good for its own sake, but no one is bad for its own sake. People only do evil for the sake of some other goal—pleasure, self-interest, revenge, rebellion, and so forth. Good, these thinkers would say, is the real thing; evil is only a parasite or a corruption of the good.

This leads us to another important point. Have you ever wondered why Jesus, the God of the whole universe, the walking, incarnate arché of being, did nothing to stop His persecutors and tormentors? He was captured, tortured, and killed—all passive things. Yet when He came back from the dead, He declared that He had defeated death, overcome the world, and conquered evil. At face value He didn't appear to *do* anything, but this is the twist: He didn't have to. If Christ had done battle with a personification of death or engaged in single combat with the devil, it might make more sense to us visually, but it would send a very different message: namely, that might makes right, that Christ defeated evil by virtue of His superior power. That would imply a problematic universe, one of no moral content at all apart from the use of power. But this is not the message of the gospel. That Jesus conquered evil and death without force is a witness to the ultimate reality of Goodness. In other words, Goodness doesn't need to use force to prove its reality if it *is* reality. This is the same reason Jesus couldn't stay dead: He is life itself, and life itself cannot die.

I think people understand this at an unconscious level. You see it in pop culture, where the hero of a story prevails in the face of an enemy that is physically more powerful than he is. Almost always the hero needs to make a sacrifice or experience a death of some kind before he's able to achieve victory, just as Christ does in the Gospel accounts. And the trope that good always defeats evil or that evil always self-destructs (for example, when the antagonists turn on each other) is not a platitude for younger readers and viewers; it's a bold statement about the ultimate nature of good and evil. No matter how much power evil appears to have or how much harm it does in the short term, evil cannot last because it is not ultimate reality; it's just a corruption. In the end, evil and suffering will be overcome and all their works undone. This is why suffering and evil are not, and cannot be, a "part of God's plan." God is not the source of evil; He is the *conqueror* of the evil *we* cause through the misuse of our freedom.

The heart of the gospel is often summed up in this phrase: "The tomb is empty." There's a reason Easter is the central holiday in Christianity. The Resurrection of Christ from the dead is the declaration that a new age has dawned. Yes, suffering and evil still linger in the world, but Christ is leading us in a glorious revolution—not merely against one or another specific instance of suffering, but against *all* suffering and evil—a cosmic revolution that will culminate in the ultimate overthrowing of all suffering, evil, and death for all time. This is the age to come that Christ is leading us into. The Greek word we translate as "gospel"—*evangelia*—means "good news," and now you have some sense of why: it's not merely good news; it's the best possible news you could imagine.

CHAPTER 10

Becoming Human

Repentance

So, you may ask, now what? If Christ has risen from the dead and reconnected us to the arché, why isn't everything fine already? Why is there still suffering and evil in the world? The answer has to do with free will. The fact that God has opened the door to communion with Him doesn't mean we're being forced to go through. Because we have free will, we can refuse to go through the door. But free will also means that even if we want to go through the door, it may not be so easy.

You see, it isn't just that we have fallen away from the arché; it's that we have built up in ourselves a resistance to being plugged back into the arché. This resistance is another way to understand the idea of sin. I know this word has frequently been abused, both by modern Christians and by their opponents, but a very practical way to understand sin is as a moral flaw—what we call a *vice* in English. Vices like anger, laziness, jealousy, hatred, or an addiction are things that separate us from each other, from God, and even from our true selves. The reason for this separation is that vices are always rooted in some sort of unreality, in the same way that evil is always a corruption of the good rather than a thing in itself. And these vices are things we have trained ourselves into, both as individuals and as a species, for thousands of years. The act of deciding to abandon all these things is called *repentance.*

Repentance may sound like a fancy religious word, but it means something extremely practical that most people are familiar with. Repentance means a kind of turning your life around—choosing to give up, for example, an addiction or bad habit. In the context of Christianity, it means entirely giving up *all* your vices and all your bad habits. This doesn't apply only to obvious shortcomings; it means rejecting every way in which you fall short, even the smallest ones. People often talk about reaching their full potential, but they don't usually mean it, because the only way to unlock your *full* potential would be to overcome every single one of your vices and shortcomings. Jesus said the same thing, in effect, when He told His disciples that He wanted them to be perfect just as God is perfect (Matthew 5:48).

Some people think this is too lofty a goal. Some might even say it sounds alien or inhuman. But think of a time when you did the right thing, said the right thing at the right time, kept your cool in a heated situation, or actually did your best at something and it went perfectly. You were probably rather pleased with yourself or grateful that things went well. What Christianity is talking about, at a very basic level, is being like that all the time—in other words, being the best possible person you could be, at every level, every minute of every day. Imagine what sort of person you could be if you weren't affected at all by negative emotions—depression, stress, anger, or anxiety—or if you weren't held back by all the bad habits and addictions that interfere with your life. Repentance is the first step along the journey to becoming that person.

There's another thing people tend to misunderstand about repentance. The way many modern Christians talk about it makes it sound like a one-time action. Their idea is if you repent—that is, say you're sorry for your sins and declare your allegiance to Christ—then you are immediately "saved" and don't have to worry any more. It's kind of like fire insurance: declaring your faith in Jesus means you are safeguarding yourself in the event that when you die, you'll go to "the good place" rather than "the bad place." In fact, the usual emphasis on the *fires* of hell makes it almost exactly like a fire insurance pitch.

The problem with this picture of repentance and salvation is that it doesn't solve the problem. If our issue is that we—as individuals, as a culture, and as the human race—have built up all kinds of deeply ingrained habits of self-conceit, hatred, pettiness, vice, and addiction, how can a single act change all that? And in practice, we see that it doesn't. People who repent in this modern fashion may experience some sort of behavior change—they may give up obvious vices like dangerous narcotics, sexual addiction, or using vulgar language—but they are not suddenly and instantly healed of all their vices. They still become afraid, fight with other people, get their feelings hurt, say mean things, lose their tempers, and so on. And they wouldn't tell you otherwise. Instead they would say that this is somehow fine, either because God will love them anyway, or because they're still forgiven, or whatnot. But surely this misses the point. The goal is to be healed, transformed, and rid of all sin and evil by which we hurt ourselves and each other. This is the promise of the gospel. An initial repentance is good—indeed, it is necessary—but the reality is that we remain far from perfect, and being dismissive about this won't get us to perfection.

This is why the early Church viewed repentance as a lifelong activity. The authors of the New Testament, for example, talk about salvation more frequently as a future state than as a present or past event. Jesus' parables are frequently about people who take action, make sacrifices, and struggle toward some future good. Jesus says that "he who endures to the end will be saved" (Matt. 10:22), and St. Paul frequently talks about salvation in terms of training and practice for athletic competition (e.g., Heb. 12:1). This is the idea on which the ancient Church was built, and one of the major roles the Church played in people's lives was providing support and help for a life of repentance. The Church is, in this sense, something like a cross between a hospital for the sick, a recovery program for the addicted, and a training ground for the athlete.

Confession and the Saints

There are many important dimensions to how the Church helps us in our life of repentance, but I want to touch on two in particular: the role of the sacraments and the witness of the saints.

As we saw in previous chapters, the sacraments are integral in connecting us back to the arché. Baptism cleanses us of our previous sins and gives us a new nature that's able to receive the arché. The Eucharist is a little piece of the arché by which we can be nourished and healed and which (among other things) restores the arché to us bit by bit. But there is another important sacrament, absolution (sometimes called "reconciliation" in the West), which is accompanied by confession. This is the act of confessing your sins and flaws to God privately, with a priest as a witness, and getting your sins absolved.

Like all important things, this practice is almost always misunderstood by people on the outside. What it looks like is that you confess your sins to the *priest* and he personally forgives you your sins, but that is not how it really works. You are confessing your sins to God, the priest is the witness to this act, and it is God who forgives and absolves you of your sin *through the medium* of the priest.

There are two important reasons that it's good to have another human being be part of this process. One is that having a real person to whom you can be accountable is vastly different from not having one, as anyone who's had to face up to a real accountability partner can tell you. Another is that priests commonly give advice during or after confession. Priests are like coaches or therapists for your spiritual life. They give you spiritual exercises to practice and provide accountability, encouragement, and strategy talk. As with mastering a musical instrument, sport, or language, there's no way to improve without practice, and for that, we need coaches or teachers of some kind. The spiritual life is no different.

The second major help that the Church offers us is the saints themselves. The idea behind the saints is that they are the people who have made it, those who have run the race and won the crowns of victory, as St. Paul says (1 Cor. 9:24–25). This means they have fully overcome all their sins, vices, and addictions and can no longer be hurt, physically or emotionally, even by death. They have, in the understanding of the Church, become *fully human*. The saints are therefore our examples and our teachers. We read the stories of their lives to see examples of what it means to overcome evil and become truly good. The saints are also our friends and helpers. Having overcome evil and death, they are alive with Christ even now, and there are many accounts of saints appearing to people to give advice, consolation, or even miraculous help. Finally, the existence of the saints is a declaration, not just of what we individually can become, but of the promise of a new kind of life in the age to come.

Once we have been reconciled to God—reconnected with the arché—we can become ourselves in a way that we aren't able to currently. This may sound mystical or weird, but I think you have a sense of this already: there are days when you aren't quite yourself, when you are thrown out of your rhythm by your vices and afflictions. When you act out of anger, jealousy, resentment, anxiety, depression, or laziness, you are in some sense less real or less true to yourself.

You could be ten times the person you are today if you didn't have any disorders, vices, addictions, or bad habits constantly interfering and trying to drag you down. When you overcome all those things fully and completely, you might say that you arrive at the most *real* version of yourself. This is what it means to become fully filled with the arché and His energy, and what the Church means by "holiness."

When you become a more real version of yourself, you also become more in touch with reality. We've talked a lot about how, because God is the arché, He is reality itself. To draw closer to God, therefore, is to draw closer to reality—not as we think it is, but as it really is. When we sin, however, we move away from God, which means moving away from reality itself. Consequently we become less real and are less in touch with reality.

People often ask, "If God is real, where is He? Why can't I see Him?" Or, "If God wants people to be saved, why doesn't He appear to them and tell them the truth?" The answers modern Christians tend to give—that God is invisible or that this is how He tests people's faith—are not very compelling, and for good reason: they're not true. The truth is that God is constantly revealing Himself to everyone, all the time—He is, after all, reality itself. It's just that we are unable to see Him fully, correctly, or even at all, to the extent that our ability to see reality is clouded. It's not that God is hidden; it's that we are blind. Another of way of putting it is that we can encounter reality only to the extent that we ourselves are real.

Many people have had various kinds of spiritual encounters in their lives—perhaps once, perhaps intermittently, or perhaps (especially) when they were younger. But if they don't continue to seek reality, then such experiences tend to fade over time, and so we naturally associate them with being younger or immature. But if you pursue a life of virtue, ruthlessly clean your soul of vices, and participate in the sacramental life of the Church, you'll begin to grow more real, draw closer to reality, and finally be able to encounter reality Himself. The saints are those people who have become fully real and see God always.

This is why the saints are so precious in the life of the Church and why they guide, teach, and inspire us. Some of the most famous saints were the original disciples of Jesus, whose miraculous feats are documented in the New Testament. Many modern Christians look on this era as a special time—a time in which miracles and wondrous things happened because of Christ's presence, but which was only a phase that passed after Christ had gone. In reality, this era was just the beginning. The Church continued to produce miracle-working saints, century after century, and has never stopped, because the door to the arché is open, and those who seek it can find it.

This isn't to say that it's easy. If you've ever tried to recover from an addiction, change a bad habit, or fully overcome a character flaw, you know that this is no simple matter; in fact, radically changing all your vices into virtues may sound impossible. But it *is* possible, it's been done countless times, and the whole Church is set up to help you in this struggle. Confession, accountability, priests, the sacraments, all the saints, your fellow Christians, and God Himself are on your side. This also means there's no reason to be depressed by your shortcomings or discouraged when you fall. Repentance as a lifestyle doesn't mean that you never fall, but that you get back up when you do. As one of the saints said, perhaps with Proverbs 24:16 in mind, "As many times as you fall, get back up, and you will be saved." This is no different from anything else in life, from learning a game to mastering a skill. Religion is simply about the greatest skill of all: becoming a human being.

PART III

Sacred and Secular

CHAPTER 11

Two Revolutions

The History of the West

If these sacramental ideas about the arché, ultimate reality, and becoming human were the foundation of the early Church, what happened to them? How did modern, non-sacramental Christianity come into existence? To answer these questions, we need to take a step back and understand the factors that shaped the world we live in. We need to step out of the water so that we can see it better.

To do that, we must review a little bit of our own story as a civilization. History is rarely tidy, but a few broad generalizations will help give context to the discussion.

If we look at Western civilization in terms of the history of its beliefs, we find that it has three major eras, each dominated by a different worldview. Scholars used to call these eras Ancient, Medieval, and Modern, but a better way to understand them is by the worldview that shaped the civilization of each era: a pagan era, a Christian era, and a secular era.

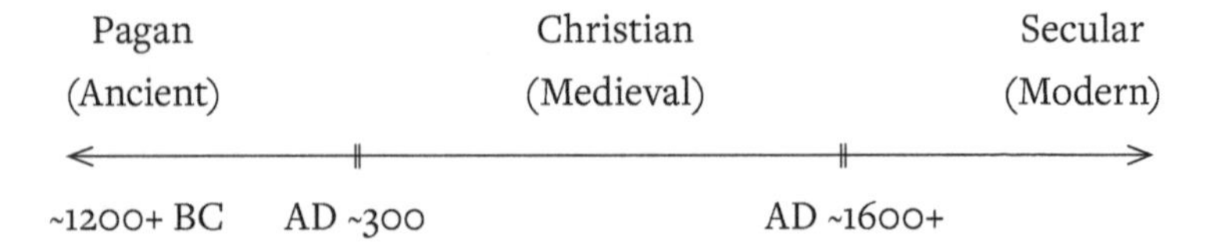

This isn't to say that there weren't people in each era who believed other things, or that there weren't variations in their beliefs. When historians talk about eras like this, they're talking about how a whole time period is formed by a particular way of thinking about the world.

The general worldview of paganism was that the world was governed by various divine beings who needed to be propitiated with sacrifices. This was the core idea around which all the major cultures of the ancient world were formed. When Christianity became the dominant worldview of the West, this kind of sacrificial system was replaced by a different way of viewing religion, one based on the new Christian ideas we discussed in the previous chapters. With the dawn of the modern era, the idea of religion itself was reworked according to a new, secular way of viewing the world. There are two major transitions, therefore, in the worldview of Western civilization: the transition from paganism to Christianity and the transition from Christianity to secularism. Let's take a brief look at each.

The First Revolution: The Dawn of Christianity

When Christianity emerged in the midst of the pagan world, it caused a tremendous and explosive revolution, not through any violent uprising, but through a radical set of new ideas that no one had ever imagined until that point. Over the course of the next few centuries, those ideas would transform the entire pagan world down to its very foundations.

At this time, most pagans believed in some conception of the arché, though they were often skeptical about their ability to interact with it or understand it very well. Then came a group of people who began insisting that the arché had somehow become a human being, not just in appearance but in nature, and that they had encountered Him and were changed by Him.

This had staggering implications. First of all, it meant that the arché could actually be encountered and known, rather than being an abstraction like a force or principle. Second, it meant that people had to rethink their idea of human nature. In a world prior to Christianity, most pagans saw the physical body as something inherently corruptible and therefore evil, and many of their religions had the goal of escaping the body and leaving it behind so that they could transcend their lowly human nature. But if the arché became fully human (rather than just taking on the *appearance* of being human), that meant that the body was not inherently evil or corrupt. Because Jesus was both God and Man, a human body was now totally joined with the arché and was therefore a part of God Himself.

This complete adoption of human nature by God bestowed a kind of radical, universal human dignity on all people, regardless of social status, sex, or ancestry. When St. Paul wrote, "There is neither Jew nor Greek, there is neither slave nor free, there is neither male nor female; for you are all one in Christ Jesus" (Gal. 3:28), it was one of the most radical things that had ever been said in human history up to that point.

Prior to the Incarnation of Christ, there was simply no reason to believe anything like this. It was obviously better to be some kinds of people than others. It was better to be free than a slave, it was safer to be male than female, and just about everyone asserted that his culture was better than his neighbor's. (Of course, some cultures *were* better than others: it was better, for example, to be a part of a culture that didn't practice human sacrifice.) But Christianity changed all this by insisting that, regardless of their physical differences, all people were equal in their radical dignity as human beings. No one in history had ever said anything like this—until God became man, there was no reason to.

The second event that transformed pagan civilization was the Resurrection. Jesus, the incarnated arché, had been put to death by His enemies, and not only did He return from the dead, but in doing so, He also conquered death itself. As if that wasn't radical enough, the early Christians explained that Jesus was now inviting all people to share in His conquering of death and evil through participation in the sacraments. Through the sacraments, Jesus became a bridge for all people to be drawn up into the life of the arché itself, so that even if they died, they would be alive in Christ—because death itself had been ultimately defeated. Christ's victory, in other words, was the beginning of a cosmic change to reality. It therefore offered an incredible hope in the face of death and evil that wasn't even conceivable prior to the advent of Christianity.

This hope was so strong that Christianity was able to endure in the face of violent persecution by the ruling powers. Brutal executions and tortures did nothing to quell its spread. On the contrary, it spread like wildfire all over the Roman Empire, until finally the Roman Emperor Constantine became a Christian and declared an end to the persecutions. This put Christianity at the heart of the empire, not simply making it the first Christian state (in a sense), but inaugurating a new era of civilization altogether. This civilization had three distinct features:

#1: Christianity Operated as a Single Family

When the emperor converted to Christianity, one of the first things he did was to call for a council to be held, to which he summoned the leaders of all the churches—the bishops—in order to define exactly what Christianity was and what it meant to be a Christian. Because Christianity had been a persecuted religion for three centuries and was therefore an underground movement, there were many issues on which Christians were not in agreement. Various controversies about Christian doctrine and practice had begun to spring up, and it was necessary for the Church to establish some kind of unanimity. The bishops met and talked for months and finally produced a universal statement of the faith, called the Nicene Creed, that defined what it meant to be a Christian. They also laid down the major rules for the organization of the Church. Going forward, Christianity was united in its beliefs and practices across the empire.

This isn't to say there weren't controversies, either at the time or in the centuries that followed, but the Church dealt with each of these major issues as a single family. Whenever a new concern arose, a council would be called, the matter would be discussed, and a decision would be reached with representatives from all the churches present to sign off on the decision—in the same way a big family might call a family meeting in order to work through some issue.

It's true that things didn't always go smoothly. Like any family, the Church was (and is) made up of flawed human beings, and so it went in and out of dysfunctional, tumultuous periods. But what mattered was that, whatever issues might come up, the Church still conceived of itself as one family and tried to deal with its issues as part of a single ongoing conversation about the place of Christian values in Western civilization.

For simplicity's sake, I'm deliberately glossing over the many complex controversies that spanned this period, especially the schism between East and West, which deserves its own separate discussion and for which there are many other resources available. But for the purpose of contrasting the Christian age to the secular one that followed, it's much more significant that all Christians at this time universally believed in and practiced some kind of sacramental theology. And even when the East and West split, and the sacramental orientation in the West began to weaken, everyone still generally believed that Christian ideas needed to be at the foundation of a shared civilization—something that was not true in the modern era that followed.[2]

#2: Religion and Government Were Not Separable

Modern people are very comfortable with the idea of a separation between Church and State, but ancient people would have had a hard time even understanding what we mean by this. You might say that this was because the Church and State had equal power when it came to organizing society, but even that is too modern a way of talking about it. For ancient people there was simply no way to divorce the question of how to run society (politics) from the question of meaning and morality (religion). Religious leaders were always at the heart of a culture's leadership, either as advisors to the king, members of ruling councils, or—in some societies—identical with the rulers themselves.

In the Christian era this concept was called *symphony. Symphony* is a word of Greek origin that means "heard together" in the sense of musical harmony. It was understood that the leaders of government positions, like kings and emperors, were responsible for the good of their people, not just physically but spiritually, and they were therefore expected to rule in harmony with the religious leaders.

Today we would call these two elements the Church and the State, but ancient people would not have thought of them as entirely separate categories. The bishops were citizens of the empire and therefore

2 For those interested in a more detailed history of Christian civilization, I highly recommend John Strickland's four-volume series, *Paradise and Utopia* (Ancient Faith Publishing, 2019–22).

subject to the rulers, but at the same time the rulers were Christians and therefore spiritually subject to the clergy. It went both ways. The traditional Byzantine image of this relationship was the two-headed eagle: the body of the eagle (the empire) had two heads that were equally important (the imperial rulers and the clergy). The clergy had the ability to call out moral wrongdoings and keep the empire in line with Christian ideas, while the emperor had the power to call councils of the Church and uphold the laws to which the bishops were subject.

#3: Christian Values Drove Cultural Progress

Modern people have a lot of strange ideas about what were considered Christian values at this time. Some people think they were about conforming to certain beliefs about science, such as the idea that the sun orbited the Earth. In fact, these were merely disputes among academics, and—contrary to the pop-culture myths about this period—they never had anything to do with essential Christian values. The actual values of Christianity are so basic to modern people that we have a hard time remembering or even imagining a time when they weren't universal.

Probably the most significant value was the Christian concept of universal human dignity. The pagan world had never put any intrinsic value on human life—it had no reason to. In pagan Rome, for example, slaves had no legal status at all, deadly blood sports were a common form of mass entertainment, and the punishments handed out to criminals would be considered cruel and unusual by modern standards. Perhaps most disturbing was the way in which infanticide was fully normalized in the Greco-Roman world, and pagans practiced it with an alarming degree of indifference toward the children they killed. Female babies especially were victims of this brutal kind of family planning, generally being seen as less desirable than male babies. But as soon as Christian values took root in the culture, this practice rapidly died out, given that it was totally incompatible with Christianity's radical compassion for all human beings.

Instead, what Christianity produced was the first institutionalized forms of charity in Western history. Christians had always viewed helping the sick and the poor as mandatory, but under the new Christian emperors, for the first time in history, government funding was set aside for charity and relief at an institutional level.

The weakening of the institution of slavery was another major change in this period. Some people are critical of the fact that Christianity didn't immediately lead to formal abolitionist movements (though it would eventually do so), but that criticism overlooks the magnitude of the change Christianity brought about in the ancient world's concept of the person.

Slavery was a universal feature of pre-modern societies. Ancient people could not really conceive of a world in which there was not a bonded class of people, as debt-based servitude and other legal bonds were practical, everyday features of their economy (as they are in our present-day world, though in different forms). What Christianity did was to change how people thought about personhood. At that time, slaves had no real legal status, or what we today would call human rights. The ancient way of putting this was that they had no "face" before the law. The way it was phrased in Latin literally meant that they were not persons in the eyes of the State.

But Christianity said otherwise. In the Church, everyone had an identity in Christ. Slaves participated with their masters as equal members in the sacramental life, and they all took the Eucharist together as brothers and sisters. This gave slaves the status of persons, one that wasn't available to them under the old way of thinking. Legal reforms under Christian emperors acknowledged this universal dignity and progressively expanded the rights of slaves beyond anything a pagan could have imagined, weakening the institution of slavery in general and eventually leading to its abolishment in many places in the world. Though it's difficult for modern people to appreciate this fully, it's impossible to overstate how unbelievable and unprecedented this transformation was. It's not an exaggeration to say that our concept of human rights would not—and *could* not—have come into existence without Christianity's revolution of the concept of the human being.

It's difficult to measure the exact cultural effect of something of this magnitude. But one thing that's very noticeable is the correlation of the new concept of human dignity with the sudden increase in technological development. Parallel to the weakening and transformation of slavery, Western culture developed an interest in technological means of labor-saving that wasn't present in previous ages.

The ancient Greeks are a good contrast. Centuries prior to Christ, they had actually invented steam engine technology, but at the time they considered it merely a curiosity. It seems that it didn't occur to them to use it as a means of labor-saving, probably because their whole civilization was founded on a slave economy. Slaves had no time to develop such technology, and the leisure class (who did have the time) simply had no need for labor-saving—they had slaves to do mundane labor. But with the rise of the concept of universal human dignity, the Medieval era would see the pioneering of a huge variety of new inventions and technological advances across every sector of life.

Another major value of Christian culture was the idea that the universe was the creation of a single, rational mind—the arché. The universe, therefore, was a fundamentally rational place that could be understood and investigated, something pagans often had a hard time trusting because of their belief in the capricious nature of the gods. The idea that there was a *unity* amidst the *diversity* of all knowledge led Christian thinkers to create the *uni-versity* system, a group of institutions where scholars and thinkers could collaborate. The universities were probably the most important invention of the Medieval period, as they rapidly became the epicenters for immense progress in science, logic, mathematics, literacy, and the arts. People often talk about the Renaissance era that followed as some sort of miraculous, sudden leap forward in academic and scientific progress, but the truth is that this period of advances was the result of centuries of groundwork laid by Medieval and Byzantine thinkers—precisely because of their religious conviction that the universe was rational. In other words—contrary to popular belief—religion was the major driving force behind the scientific advances of this era.

The Second Revolution: The Protestant Reformation

If you've had any kind of historical education in the last hundred years, you probably learned a particular story about Western religion. The story is that, by the 1500s, the Western church had become hopelessly corrupt, and a heroic monk named Martin Luther rose up and demanded that the church reverse its wayward practices. His call for reform led to the Protestant Reformation, which succeeded in breaking the Western church's corruption and putting Christianity back on the right track.

Unfortunately, this is not what actually happened. In reality, the Reformation heralded the end of twelve centuries of Christian civilization and dealt a wound to Christian culture from which it has never recovered.

Let's start with what's true about the Reformation narrative. It's true that Western Christianity was in need of reform, but what is not widely known is that for the past several centuries, the Western church had been in an ongoing state of reform—what are called the papal reforms. Though seemingly well-intentioned, these reforms were causing their own kinds of problems, some of which were quite serious.

But the Reformation didn't solve these problems; it only made them worse. This was partly because of how radical it was. The Reformation wasn't merely a program of reform; it was a revision of the core principles of Christianity, principles that had been central to the Church for its entire existence up until that point. There were many factors in this colossally significant period of history, and Luther has been the subject of much scholarly analysis and debate, but I think we can fairly generalize three major consequences of Luther's revolution:

#1: Denial of the Authority of the Councils of the Church

By far Luther's most radical position was that not only were specific practices of the historical Church in need of an update, but *all the councils of the Church were invalid.* To appreciate this, you have to understand how significant the councils were. Whenever an issue came up in Christianity, the whole Church would meet and discuss the issue, often for many months, and then come to a conclusion that everyone agreed on and that would then be normative for the entire Church. This is how any organization has to function, of course, or it couldn't function at all. But if none of the decisions the Church had made throughout history up to Luther's time were valid, then practically speaking, Christianity in its entirety was up for revision. This was not a simple matter of reform; it was, practically speaking, an invitation to create a new religion.

#2: The Divorce of Scripture from Tradition

What then would be the foundation for this new Christianity? Luther proposed that the ultimate authority in Christianity should be the Bible. The Bible had always been authoritative in Christianity, but as we saw in previous chapters, other components were just as authoritative, especially the liturgy and the councils. All of these were seen as parts of apostolic Tradition, and all were vital in the life of the Church. When the Reformers rejected the other parts of apostolic Tradition, however, the Bible was left as the only remaining authority to guide Christianity, and so it began to take on a new status as the supreme authority for Christian life and teaching.

It's important to realize that the Bible had never been understood in this way at *any previous point* in Christian history. Least of all did the early Church understand the Bible this way, as it didn't even have a complete canon of Scripture for its first three centuries. But now the Bible suddenly needed to become a completely self-sufficient package to guide every aspect of Christian life. It needed to do all the work previously done by the Nicene Creed, the councils, the liturgy, and the rest of apostolic Tradition—by itself. As you might expect, this new way of understanding the Bible created a massive shift in what Christianity was about. Christianity was no longer—in the same direct, sacramental way—about a Man; it was now about a book.

There are many problems with the shift to the Bible as the sole authority for Christianity. We've talked about most of them in previous chapters, especially how Scripture and Tradition can't be separated in any way that makes sense. But the real proof is practical. The problem with making the Bible the sole, authoritative standard for Christianity was simply that it didn't work. If the Bible were perfectly clear, self-interpreting, and able to stand on its own without the rest of Apostolic Tradition, then what we'd expect to see following the Reformation would be a movement toward greater unity among Christians. But, of course, this is precisely the opposite of what happened. There was an immediate explosion of new and incompatible interpretations of Christianity, ones that differed not on small, trivial issues but on massive, systemic issues such as which books belong in the Bible, whether (and which of) the sacraments are real, and even whether God is a Trinity.

When everything in theology becomes open for interpretation in this way, it changes the tenor of the religion. Modern Christianity became, from the beginning of the Reformation, a problem of *knowledge*. It became focused on trying to figure out the right theology among a whole host of competing theologies. Whereas ancient Christians read the Bible for edification as part of the yearly cycle of the liturgical calendar, modern Christians studied the Bible in order to distinguish right theology from potentially wrong theology—and came to radically differing conclusions. Christianity, in other words, no longer operated as a single family; it was hopelessly fragmented into tens of thousands of competing denominations. The end result was that religion started to become a matter of personal opinion rather than the shared cultural fabric of Western civilization.

#3: The Removal of Christianity from the Heart of Society

The possibility of creating your own religion had immediate political appeal. Having a symphony of cooperation between rulers and religious leaders is convenient if you want a society fundamentally ordered by Christian values. But it's very inconvenient if you are someone in a position of power who would rather not be held morally accountable for your actions. Given the growing wealth and power of the European rulers at the time (and the various frustrations, resentments, and fears caused by the past few hundred years of political instability), political leaders had an increasing desire to remove the Church's ability to hold the State accountable. And people realized that they couldn't be held morally accountable to religious authorities if they weren't members of the same religion.

The most straightforward example of this is England's King Henry VIII. Put briefly, Henry was dissatisfied with his marriage because his wife was not producing male offspring, and he needed an heir to the throne. His plan was to get an annulment of the marriage—a kind of technicality that functionally resulted in a divorce—in the hopes of marrying another woman who would bear him sons. The Bishop of Rome, however, would not grant him this, because divorce—functional or otherwise—was not in keeping with a Christian understanding of marriage. So Henry appointed his own bishop in England who *would* grant the annulment. Henry then began restructuring the laws of England in a way that separated England from the Roman church and functionally created its own church. The head of this new Church of England would (conveniently) be the monarch of England—in other words, Henry himself and the heirs to his throne. He was no longer of the same religion as the Bishop of Rome and therefore couldn't be held morally accountable to him.

This sort of thing would continue to happen throughout the Western world for the next century. Such events cumulatively led to the creation of an entirely new sociopolitical order. New churches were started constantly, all over the West, and those denominational differences were quickly co-opted by various national and private interests that had much to gain in terms of their own power.

The bitter rivalries between competing groups led to what are called the Wars of Religion of the early modern period. While these conflicts were long and complex, the collective fallout was that Europe no longer had a shared, standard set of religious values. Almost every European country ended up either establishing its own national religion from one of the new denominations (as with Lutheranism in Germany), or else reducing the traditional religion of their country to an extension of the State (as with Catholicism in France).

In previous eras there had been a universal character to the Western world. Even if Italians and Germans and English and French people differed culturally, they all shared something that could unite them at the level of the most important issues: their worldview. But with religion redistributed along nationalist lines, Europe became a fragmented collection of rival states without any shared identity or common authority to which they could appeal. Religion became an extension of the State, and religious intolerance became a powerful weapon used by governments to enforce nationalist loyalty or conformity to the State—not because religion was the supreme power in the land, but because the State was.

The discovery of the New World brought hope to the hearts of many people who wanted to practice their version of Christianity in peace. Representatives of a number of denominations sailed west to the Americas to establish what we might call the first religiously neutral nation in history. The United States of America was seen by some people as the ultimate expression of a free society precisely because it was founded on neutrality toward religious denominations, rather than the State taking sides and endorsing one particular denomination. While it affirmed the existence of a supreme deity, the United States did not go far beyond this into any particular doctrinal statements about things like the sacraments or the Trinity but left the exact interpretation of these ideas up to the individual religions, and ultimately to individual persons. The State would be neutral toward nearly all religious doctrine. Or, to put it another way, it would be *secular.*

The continuing proliferation of denominations within nations would lead, in just a few generations, to religion being ultimately reduced to a matter of personal opinion. There was no longer any shared morality to draw on. This paved the way for the rise of secularism as the dominant worldview of the Western world. Along with it came the conditions that would lead to an entirely new kind of Christianity.

CHAPTER 12

Secularism and Christianity

The Birth of the Secular State

What is secularism? The word has been used in different ways throughout history, but for the purpose of our discussion, secularism is the idea that the government—and indeed, the functioning of society at large—should be conducted without any involvement of religion or religious beliefs.

In order to do this, Western civilization had to establish a completely new way of thinking about the world. We discussed this in chapter five: viewing the physical and the spiritual world as separate realities—and therefore categorizing all knowledge as either objective or subjective rather than participatory. While there had been a trend among Western philosophers toward this kind of thinking for the past few centuries, it wasn't until the modern era that these ideas really became the basis on which to structure society. Or, more accurately, it was precisely the shift to these ideas that marked the end of the old Christian civilization and heralded the beginning of the modern era.

You might argue that the division between the physical and the spiritual was made permanent in people's imaginations by the religious controversies of this era. After the Reformation and the breakdown of religion in Europe, no one could agree on spiritual matters. The only thing people had in common was the reality of the physical world. This is also why it was attractive to abandon a participatory way of thinking in favor of dividing knowledge into the objective and the subjective. Because objective things could be measured and therefore proven, people could agree on them regardless of their spiritual beliefs. This led to a loss of interest in those things that couldn't be proven. Not just religion, but art, morality, and meaning in general gradually became reclassified as subjective, meaning they were reduced to matters of personal opinion. The goal of all this was to create a religiously neutral society, what historians call the secular nation state.

If you grew up in one of these cultures, this may not sound like a problem to you. That's because we've been taught that religious neutrality is possible and even desirable. Even if you're religious, you might not see anything wrong with allowing religion to be a matter of personal opinion. Anything beyond that probably sounds like forcing your religion on other people. This all sounds very kind and tolerant, but when we're talking about worldview, this type of thinking quickly breaks down. Contrary to what we've been told, it isn't possible to have a neutral worldview—and in fact, trying to have one leads to serious issues.

The Fallacy of Neutrality

While you can be neutral about many things, worldview is not one of them. This is because you can't answer the question "How should we govern society?" without having a solid answer to the question "What is the nature of ultimate reality?" This may sound a little dramatic, but it's actually very basic.

It's a simple fact that you can't take care of something without knowing what it is. If I asked you, "How do you best care for a *hymenopus coronatus*?" you couldn't give me an answer without knowing what exactly a hymenopus coronatus is. Humanity is no different. How do you best organize a human society? That depends on what we think a human is. We need to have some understanding of human nature in order to organize a human society. But as soon as we start asking questions about human nature, we need to ask more fundamental questions about the nature of things like personhood and morality. Before you know it, we're asking all the big questions of religion—the questions of ultimate reality.

It turns out you can't run a society without answering the question of ultimate reality. You can try to ignore the question, as secular society does, on the basis that it's "religious," but then you're saying something else: you're saying that the question—by definition—isn't important. If it were actually important, it couldn't be ignored.

Another way of putting this is that, if you really believed something was the highest truth—in other words, the *most important*—you would make that thing the foundation of your entire culture and way of life. The reverse is also true: If you don't make something the foundation of your entire culture, then you are implicitly saying that it isn't the highest or most important truth. If you exclude religion from the foundation of your culture, you're sending the message that religion itself is of no ultimate importance.

But of course, none of this is actually neutral. You can't be neutral when you're asking questions about the nature of reality. If you say that religion isn't ultimately important to the way we run society, you're making a non-neutral statement about how the world works. You're saying, in other words, that at least one other worldview is wrong—namely, the sacramental or enchanted view of the world, which says the physical and the spiritual can't be separated.

And if you say someone is wrong, you aren't being neutral. In fact, if you think about it, you'll realize that there is no such thing as a neutral worldview, because every statement you make *about the world* is a worldview.

The Breakdown of Secularism

Instead of giving a single answer to the question of ultimate reality, secular thinkers thought they could have a more free and neutral society if they simply let everyone give their own answer to the question. Worldview would be reduced to a matter of personal opinion, as though it were another kind of consumer choice. But of course, that is not what religion is. Having a religion means having a worldview, an answer to the question, "What is the nature of ultimate reality?"

This is not a trivial question. It is by definition the ultimate question; it affects everything about everything. A society in which people are left alone to choose their own favorite pizza toppings is one thing; you cannot treat the question of ultimate reality in the same way. While there are no serious consequences of everyone making different consumer choices, if everyone chooses a different worldview, then you quickly produce a culture in which we don't agree on all the most important issues. This inevitably results in fragmentation, antagonism, and instability.

But in order for a society to function, it needs some kind of stability. In a secular society, that stability is provided by the State. But this leads to serious issues, because the secular nation state—precisely because it is secular—cannot provide a basis for real morality.

As we discussed in chapter nine, the fact that we like or approve of something doesn't make it morally good. "We all agree on this," "because I said so," and "this is in everyone's best interest" are not statements about the true moral reality of the cosmos; they're just statements about whatever we're trying to do. For something to be morally good—Good with a capital "G"—it has to be higher than anyone's personal opinions, the consensus of a people, or the decrees of a government. Absolute morality, in other words, is always based on the ultimate meaning of things—and meaning requires the integration of the spiritual with the physical.

By definition, the secular nation state is a type of government that rejects the spiritual. In such a system, our behavior isn't directed by higher moral realities; it's ordered by whatever the State says and ultimately by what the State chooses to enforce through punishments and rewards—in a word, it's ordered by whoever has power. But if morality is merely a function of power, then you don't have a moral society at all; you have an amoral one.

It's no surprise that the increasing power of the secular nation states in the modern era ultimately culminated in the catastrophes of the twentieth century. From the massacres of the communist revolutions to the devastation of the world wars, from the brutality of the internment camps to the horror that was the atomic bomb, the twentieth century was the most violent, blood-soaked period in human history—not by a little, but by orders of magnitude. And what else would you expect from a world in which the secular nation states—of whatever kind—were answerable to no moral authority higher than their own self-interest?

These issues, like all issues, ultimately stem from worldview. Secularism's worldview—its answer to the question of ultimate reality—is that the physical world is the primary or only reality and that objective knowledge is the only or most reliable kind of knowledge. Therefore, participatory knowledge, the spiritual world, ultimate meaning, and even morality itself are not important when it comes to running society.

Sacramental Christianity in a Secular Age

This isn't to say that every secular culture is somehow inherently wicked. People in these societies, as well as their governments, do good all the time. Despite its secularism, many good things have come out of modern culture, and while I think there are also important practical critiques of the secular nation state, they're not important for the main point of this discussion. In exploring the origins and beliefs of secularism, what we're trying to understand is how (and why) different cultures think about the world so we can be more aware of how our own culture influences our thinking.

When secular thinking becomes the dominant worldview, it creates a culture in which it is difficult or impossible to see the world in a sacramental way. The idea that physical things—like the water in baptism or the bread and wine in Communion—can contain or communicate spiritual realities makes no sense in this view. The idea that you can actually participate in the cosmic liturgy by imitating it, or that the spiritual power of Jesus' original disciples could be passed down by physical touch through a succession of priests, or that objects can contain special spiritual energy—all these things are incomprehensible in a worldview that divides the physical from the spiritual. The idea that we can't see God because we aren't yet fully real also doesn't fit into secularism, as there can't be any higher reality if the physical world is the only reality (or the only one that matters). If objective knowledge is the only valid kind of knowledge, then moral growth is irrelevant to intellectual growth, and the idea that truth is a Person is simply nonsensical.

These incompatibilities explain much of our religious culture. It's common, for example, to encounter people who sincerely want to be Christians but who don't understand—or who outright reject—the core ideas of sacramental Christianity. It isn't because they're bad people; it's because their way of thinking about the world has been shaped by secularism, and—as with the Irish converts from paganism—it's difficult to change how you think about the world all at once.

Some people think that belonging to a sacramental tradition makes you immune to these dangers, but that's to assume you're above the influence of your own cultural context, which is never true. That doesn't mean it's impossible to live out sacramental lives and learn to think in a sacramental way while living in a secular world; it just means we have to be more careful and more diligent. I think there are a few important things to keep in mind as we try to work out our faith in a culture whose worldview is fundamentally hostile to our own.

#1: Internalize the Relationship between the Physical and the Spiritual

To fully participate in the sacramental life means you have to internalize, fundamentally, the belief that the spiritual and the physical are inseparable. They are not two different levels of reality but are completely integrated—physical objects and actions genuinely allow you to interact with spiritual realities.

At some level, despite whatever we say, modern people (almost by definition) struggle with this. We've been taught our whole lives that the physical is just the physical, and the spiritual, if it exists, is somewhere else: it's invisible, or it's far away, or it's "in heaven." Even a modern person who believes in miracles probably thinks of the physical world as primary and the miracle as an exception that temporarily suspends the laws of physics; then everything goes back to being purely physical after the miracle is over. But to think sacramentally is much bigger than this. It doesn't mean thinking that only certain objects or actions have spiritual significance; it means realizing that the entire physical world has spiritual content, and the reason you can't see most (or any) of it is that you aren't yet fully human.

#2: Realize that You Are a Work in Progress

There is a common misconception that the main goal of religion is to have the correct beliefs, and that all you need to do to be a real Christian or to be saved is to hold the right combination of beliefs with the appropriate level of sincerity. This is why the usual question in these kinds of religions is "Do you believe in Jesus?" But of course, belief is not enough. Even the demons believe, as St. James reminds us (James 2:19), but that doesn't save them.

The reality is that belief is the first part of a three-step process. Having the right beliefs is good—in fact, it's necessary—but it's only the first step. The second step is to put those beliefs into action, and then to repeat those actions regularly enough that you end up transforming into a certain kind of person. In order to become physically healthy, for example, you first have to believe that you need to go to the gym, and then you have to put that belief into practice by going to the gym, not once, but regularly. Only with time and patience do you become healthy.

Again, the problem with being cut off from the arché is not that we have the wrong beliefs (although that may also be true). The main problem is that we are cut off from that which is Goodness and Life itself. This is why Orthodox Christians don't talk about "being saved" as the moment when we came to accept certain ideas about Jesus. That would be like saying, "The moment I bought a gym membership I was instantly healthy." It's true that buying a gym membership may have been the moment in which you began your path toward being healthy, but to equate the two is to confuse intentions with results.

#3: Accept that Your Task Is to Be Taught by the Church, Not Vice Versa

Another issue related to overemphasizing belief is the temptation to think that your individual knowledge is higher than the whole sum of Orthodox Tradition. This affliction can manifest in different ways. You might pick fights with people on the internet over the correct interpretation of doctrine, or feel the need to correct or control the behavior of others. You might decide that you disagree with the councils of the Church, or start a movement to overturn a tradition that's hundreds (or even thousands) of years old because it doesn't match what you think Christianity should look like. You could also decide that certain practices, traditions, or ideas need to be added to the life of the Church and that you are the one to do so.

On the other hand, your concerns might be less intellectual. You might believe that your spiritual feelings are more primary than the Church, or that what God "tells" you personally is somehow more real or more important than the liturgy, the councils, or the guidance of your confessor.

None of these is an Orthodox way of thinking. For one thing, we don't prioritize the intellect as the path to God. It isn't that the intellect is bad—we have many beautiful saints who were, for lack of a better word, intellectual geniuses. But the more Orthodox path is to realize that real understanding is participatory—it requires moral formation. Evagrius, one of the early Church Fathers, defined a theologian not as someone who had mastered intellectual ideas about theology but as "one who prays truly." To acquire real knowledge is to know truth Himself, and that necessitates acquiring some measure of holiness.

As for personal spiritual feelings, it's important to take a humble attitude and balance them against the teachings of the Church and the input of your confessor. There have been many sad episodes in history when people have been led astray, sometimes very badly, because they thought God was talking to them. A personal relationship with God is a beautiful thing, but you can't put your relationship with Christ on one side and the Church on the other—that is a contradiction. As St. Augustine put it, "No one can have God for his Father who does not have the Church for his mother." Knowing God, in other words, isn't separable from acquiring the mind of the Church. Otherwise you're just making up your own religion—with yourself at the center.

#4: Make the Church the Center of Your Entire Life

The way you acquire the mind of the Church is by participating in the life of the Church. This doesn't just mean attending the liturgy once a week; it means making your entire life liturgical. You do this by immersing yourself in the liturgical calendar as much as you reasonably can: attending other services throughout the week, celebrating feast days, and participating in fasting periods. It's vital also that you bring the liturgical life of the Church into your home by setting up a home altar—what is commonly called a prayer corner—with icons, candles, and perhaps incense, as a place where you pray. By doing so you make your home into a miniature church—one that's connected to and participates in the liturgical life of the whole Church. You're effectively turning your entire life into a kind of liturgy with a regular rhythm of prayer, one whose whole purpose is to draw you up into the higher spiritual reality of liturgical time.

By contrast, if you make religion merely one part of your life rather than the heart of your life, that means it's not really your worldview; it's just a hobby or social activity. The Roman Catholic mystic Thomas Merton said that "a life is either all spiritual or not spiritual at all." This doesn't mean that if you're not living a perfect life you aren't a Christian or anything like that. His point wasn't to condemn but to encourage us with the idea that everything in our life can be made spiritual. Another way to put this is that you are secular to the extent that the spiritual life isn't integrated into everything you do and are, because the essence of being secular is to separate the spiritual from the physical.

#5: Don't Allow Worldly Concerns to Become Your Main Worldview

One of the constant dangers—in every era, but perhaps especially in ours—is allowing some particular issue, concern, movement, or philosophy to take the place of the gospel in your life. This can happen very subtly, even to the most well-meaning of people, so it's something for us all to be on our guard about. It generally starts with someone endorsing a particular political or cultural movement because it has some overlap with Christianity, but gradually that movement starts to displace Christianity as one's main way of viewing the world.

For example, I might see American liberalism as a good political option because of its emphasis on compassion. But because (let's say) I interact with a lot of liberal media, my constant exposure to compassion-related issues starts to influence my thinking about Christianity: over time, I come to see compassion as the most important aspect of Christianity. I focus more on those parts of the Bible or episodes in the lives of the saints that are about compassion, at the expense of other elements of Christianity. Because I've now reduced Christianity to a single issue, and that issue lines up so well with liberalism, eventually I start to see liberalism as the only valid political option for a Christian.

If this thinking gets rooted strongly enough, a switch can occur. Instead of seeing a sacramental Christian life as the goal and certain liberal policies as potential means, I unconsciously start viewing a liberal social order as the goal and Christianity as a justification for it. Liberalism, in other words, becomes the center of my worldview and Christianity just one component of my liberalism. This puts me in a bad position, as I'm now forced to downplay or ignore the explicitly anti-Christian elements of liberalism, such as its views on unborn children, human nature, and sexuality. I may even come to accept those views and try to change my definition of Christianity to include them—the ultimate sign that liberalism has become my primary worldview.

Of course, the same thing can happen with American conservatism. I could see conservatism as a good political option because of its emphasis on traditional morality and family values. But because (let's say) I listen to a lot of conservative podcasts, the same gradual shift occurs. Eventually I end up thinking that conservatism is the only valid political option for a Christian, and I view a "real conservative" and a "real Christian" as identical. But then I'm also in a bad position. Besides confusing the eternal truths of the gospel with a transitory political affiliation, I have to downplay or ignore the explicitly anti-Christian elements present in conservatism, such as its tolerance of exploitative economic arrangements, especially corporate and banking abuses.

And of course these two positions aren't the only ideas that could displace the gospel. This subtle switch can happen with any political movement, cultural issue, or philosophical system. The danger is the same.

It's easy to disregard such examples as fanciful or to think you're above these sorts of errors. But it is a much easier trap to fall into than you might think because of how gradually and unconsciously these temptations creep in. It's important to be on your guard when interacting with politics, because thinking you're immune to something is a great way to get caught in it.

This isn't to say, of course, that there is no good in any of these political movements or philosophies. There is some good in everything, as we saw in chapter nine. But it's a mistake to give such worldly issues equal importance with the gospel. There is no movement, no combination of laws, and no worldly leader that can solve our deepest problems, not because worldly things are of no importance, but because our ultimate problems as a species—sin and death—are not worldly but cosmic.

How do we stay focused on these ultimate concerns? This is what we'll explore in the final chapter.

CHAPTER 13

The Journey to Reality

The Life of the Age to Come

How does a sacramental Christian live in the age of secularism? While it's essential that we be on guard against secular influences, we shouldn't therefore live in a constant state of fear and agitation, as though our primary aim in life is to avoid being secular.

While it's obviously bad to be caught in secular thinking, to make your whole life about being *anti*-secular is also a distraction. Hating the bad is not our goal; our goal is to love the good. We are trying to reconnect to the arché and become fully human. There is no other way to fix the ultimate problems of life. That's why our focus has to be bigger than any worldly issue. It has to be toward a higher vision of reality, toward what Jesus called the Kingdom of heaven.

Modern people often refer to heaven as the afterlife, but I want to get away from the stereotypical idea of heaven. Many people, myself included, grew up with an idea of heaven as either a place of eternal rest and comfort—playing a harp while sitting on a cloud—or else a place of total hedonistic pleasure, where you'll get to do whatever you want forever. Neither of these is a Christian idea. Like most of our typical ideas of hell, these pictures of heaven are almost entirely the fantasies of pop culture and have no meaningful relation to the gospel.

I think most people have a sense of the emptiness of these images. When you're told that heaven is a place of absolute, unending pleasures, but you're told not to indulge in that kind of lifestyle here on earth, it sends a mixed message about the place of pleasure and happiness and confuses people about whether pleasure is good or bad. On the other hand, if you tell a child that heaven consists mostly of resting, singing, or just standing in the presence of God, you'll excite nothing in his spirit except boredom. This is why young people sometimes say things like, "Heaven is boring. I want to go to hell, where all the interesting people are going to be." Though this is ultimately a foolish thing to say, the error is not entirely the young person's fault; it's the fault of the people who told him the opposite of the gospel.

It's helpful to think of heaven less as a place and more as an age. This is why the Church's language in the Nicene Creed is that Christians "look for the resurrection of the dead and the life of the *age* to come" (my emphasis). This passage is sometimes translated "life of the *world* to come," but in the original Greek the word is *aeon*, which means "age," not "world." Entering the Kingdom of heaven isn't like living on planet Earth and then dying and being reborn on another, better planet called "heaven." The idea is that, with the return of Christ and the final defeat of all death and evil, a new *era* will begin for the whole cosmos.

What will this new era be like? No one can say for sure, given the nature of the thing we're talking about, but there are four important ideas to keep in mind: (1) the age to come is a *beginning*, not an end; (2) it's *more real* than this world, not less; (3) it's both *present and future*; and (4) it's *dynamic*, not static.

(1) The Beginning

The last book of the Bible is called the Revelation of John, as it was a spiritual vision the Apostle John had toward the end of his life. The vision depicts Jesus' return to earth—what's called the Second Coming of Christ—in which He defeats all evil and redeems heaven and earth. Because the original Greek-derived word for revelation is *apocalypse*, many people think of Christ's Return as the end of the world and have a hard time thinking beyond that (after all, what comes after the end?). But if you want to understand the age to come, it's better to think about the apocalypse as the *beginning*.

When God created the universe, His intention was to have a loving relationship with creation. But when mankind used its free will to walk out of relationship with God, disconnecting itself from the arché and bringing death and corruption into the world, mankind went off course from the original plan God had laid out for us. Imagine you begin to walk somewhere, but you take a wrong turn and get very lost. You spend a long time trying to get back to the street you were on, and only then can you really begin traveling to your destination. In this way, the whole history of the human race—and of Christ's coming to conquer death and reopen the path to the arché—is more like a course correction, putting us back on track. You would never call the course correction the *end* of the journey. It's still the beginning, except now you're on the right path.

(2) Journey to the Real

Where are we going, you may ask? The short answer is something like "to reality." We are drawing closer to the arché, and with that comes the fullness of the reality that we now experience only partially. This is what St. Paul meant when he said that now we see "dimly," but then (in the age to come) we shall see "face to face" (1 Cor. 13:12). This is the deeper meaning of the word *apocalypse*. In Greek, this word doesn't just mean a revelation in the sense that St. John had a vision; it means something closer to "unveiling" in the sense that the veil between us and God will be removed. I can't say what it will be like to see God face to face, but the language of the saints is that—through our sacramental union with Christ—we actually become participants in the life of the Holy Trinity. We will be fully plugged into Life and Love Himself.

It's important to understand the place of pleasure and happiness here. Talking about heaven as a place of infinite indulgence in pleasure is infantile. Maximizing the amount of dopamine in your brain is not what we're talking about; there's a reason that people who live only for pleasure inevitably become depressed and miserable.

It's better to talk about what we might call *joy*. We've all had experiences that elicit a sense of happiness and meaning that transcends mere pleasure; it's something that touches on a deep feeling of reality, something that fills you up in a way mere pleasure cannot.

This distinction is at the heart of why the Church has always cautioned people against being too caught up in earthly pleasures. Many people mistakenly think that this is because the Church is against pleasure and fun and wants everyone to be boring and miserable. I saw this best expressed in my childhood when some authority figure would ask, "Do you love video games (or sports, or ice cream, etc.), or do you love *God*?" And of course, you're supposed to say "God," but this is difficult, especially when you're young, because the video games (or sports or ice cream) are tangible, concrete realities, and God is much more abstract.

This is why it's so important to understand God as the arché. There is a prayer in the Orthodox tradition that describes God as the "treasury of every good," meaning that God Himself, in His being, is like a room full of treasure chests that contain not merely good things, but *every good thing*. This makes sense when you understand that God is both being itself and goodness itself, making Him the source and origin of *all good*. This is also why Jesus tells us to seek first the Kingdom of heaven, and then everything else will be added to us (Matt. 6:33)—not because the Kingdom of heaven is *better*, but because the Kingdom of heaven is *everything there is*. This is no reality apart from it.

In that sense, the issue is more about distinguishing between the source and the things that come *from* the source. It would be much more accurate to say something like, "Don't get so caught up in a lesser good (such as video games, sports, or ice cream) that you forget where goodness comes from." The mistake is to think that real joy comes from the thing you happen to be enjoying in the moment. The truth is that joy comes *through* those things from the source of all Joy and Goodness itself—the arché.

Another way of saying this is that you get a little taste of the ultimate joy of the age to come in all the little samples of joy that you encounter in your day-to-day experience. It would be a mistake to focus on those things you encounter (eating, playing, experiencing) as though they were good in themselves; they merely remind you of the source of all good. For example, if you love dogs, you get some joy from watching a video of a dog. But that's not because you love the video; it's because you love dogs. The video only gives you any joy because it reminds you of the thing you really love.

This is why all the great religious traditions have always incorporated some kind of fasts or other limitations on the basic pleasures of life. The reason the Church puts restrictions on pleasures (such as eating, drinking, and sex) is not that she is against them, but she wants you to be able to distinguish between lesser, derivative goods and Goodness itself.

It's not, as C. S. Lewis put it, that God finds our desires too strong and therefore needs to restrict us. It's that He finds our desires too *weak*. We are too easily distracted by lesser pleasures that are ultimately transitory, when we should instead be focused on the source of all good and the joy and meaning (deeper than any mere pleasure) that come from it.

To put it a third way, the joy that you feel in your favorite thing is only a shadow of the real thing as it is (or will be) in the age to come. What you actually love about that thing is that it tastes like the fullness of reality into which the arché is calling you. These things contain a hint or a shadow; they call to you and beckon you. The reason you love the things you love is that contained in each one of them is a crumb of the real goodness of reality itself—a reality that is not yet fully here but is coming.

(3) Both Present and Future

This gets us to the idea that the age to come is both present and future. It's future in the sense that it's the next age that's coming after this one, but it's present in the sense that we can experience it partially right now. The main way we experience the age to come is by participating in the sacramental life of the liturgy. Remember that in the liturgy, all time is present—not just the past but the future as well. To be in the liturgy is not just to participate along with all other Christians throughout all of history, but also to encounter a small taste (what the Church calls a "foretaste") of the next age.

The technical term for this phenomenon is *proleptic*—it means "already" and "not yet" at the same time. You see hints of this in the New Testament when Jesus says both that the Kingdom of heaven is coming (Mark 1:15) *and* that it's already "within you" (Luke 17:21); and when He tells the Samaritan woman that "the time is coming *and* has now come" (John 4:23 NIV, my emphasis). You might say we're standing in the transition between two ages: we have one foot in the present age, but we're dipping our toes into the age to come. And we participate in the fullness of that reality to the extent that we ourselves have become real.

(4) Dynamic Life

Finally, the age to come is the beginning of a new kind of era. What will we do in that era? Again, we can only speculate, but we can at least get rid of this idea of a static heaven where people simply rest or enjoy themselves, as though the age to come were some sort of perpetual Saturday of lounging around or partying. If the age to come is a new beginning, then my guess is that it will be very much like this life: there will be projects, adventures, challenges, and great deeds to do. It's hard to remember in our overworked society, but the human person actually needs and enjoys work—provided that the work has real meaning. This is why I think so many people play sports or difficult games or undertake complex projects as their recreation. There's something intrinsically meaningful in building, creating, learning, and striving. These things are part of our being, so we can expect that they will be a part of the age to come.

In any case, the age to come will not be boring. As far as I can tell, it will consist of people operating at their full potential, striving for great and meaningful things, without sin, death, vice, sickness, or evil to interfere at all. Imagine the world as you know it, but perfected: everyone is fully plugged into the arché and is part of one giant family, so there's no hatred or hostility. Everyone has a job that is full of meaning. Everyone is growing and working together, playing and eating together, planning great plans, starting new projects, inventing new things, going on adventures, and working together.

The dawn of the age to come is a new beginning with the world as it was meant to be, and we will still have to make it. But it will be a joy and an adventure, the kind of glorious adventure we all love to fantasize about through books or movies. Except it will be real. Indeed, it will be reality itself.

About the Author

Zachary Porcu is a professor of history and theology at the University of St. Katherine in San Marcos, California, and a catechist at St. Andrew Orthodox Church in Riverside. He earned his PhD in church history from the Catholic University of America and holds degrees in philosophy, classics, and interdisciplinary humanities. You can follow his publications and talks at zacharyporcu.com.

Milton Keynes UK
Ingram Content Group UK Ltd.
UKHW012023290224
438689UK00004B/254